Ana Lydia Chavez is a mother of two young women of ages 29 and 25. She is married to Alvaro Melgoza. She was born in San Luis Rio Colorado, a small town south of the border of Yuma Arizona. She and her family migrated from there during the summer of 1977 to California, and have lived in California for over 42 years. She graduated from Fresno State in 2015 and currently is a real estate agent.

To:
My daughters, Victoria and Laura
And:
My nieces, Krystel Eve, Eva Michelle, Emma; and my only nephew, Zeke.

To my daughters, nieces and nephews. You are all so young, bright, and beautiful. I used to be like all of you. We are all different people, of course. And you might not make the same mistakes I did when I was your age, but I do not want to leave this world without sharing my life story with you. Although this story is no Twilight, full of suspense and surreal scenes, or like Harry Potter with wizards and magic, this story is the real thing, and it may or may not help you. But I feel obligated to share with you details about me. Some of which do not make me proud of who I was when younger. Although, because I recognized my flaws, it helped make me a better person. I'm also ashamed of what I have done and apologize beforehand to all of you if I offend you by sharing this with you. I just want you to understand that I mean no harm to anyone at all by writing this. Also, I want you to know that I felt, at times, that my life was not going to get any better. But now I know it was because I did not permit myself to heighten my life. I made many decisions without a thought process whatsoever, until the consequences arrived and sometimes not learning from those lessons.

Yes, there are many things in my past that I'm not proud of. However, there are some of which I am. Let me tell you, those few adjustments that I made in my life have helped me a great deal. One of them, which was by far, the most important, something about it.

It took me a while to overcome that fear of being alone. I have learned to overcome many other fears, like standing up for my rights as an individual and be outspoken. That is why I had the courage to sit down and started to write this book, knowing full well my writing skills and vocabulary were not as profound as those of other writers. But this is how I convinced myself; I was to accept and love myself for who I was. The second was to believe that I was worthy of obtaining all of my goals, and the third was to learn to love my family unconditionally.

Like I said before, in this book, you may not find what you find in other books that may use fancy writing to describe one idea and paint pictures in your mind with all the comparisons and different metamorphic expressions, as other authors use. What I know you will find, though, is the honest and true confession of a Mexican woman who was brought to the United States and learned rather quickly to grow up fast. My teenage years were not similar to other students in my school. I worked in the summers, purchased my own clothes, and very quickly became an adult with many responsibilities. It took me a long time to accept that

I was literally lost in my way of thinking. I always wanted to be a wife; have a house with a nice husband and two children. But after my first marriage, that portrait became tarnished, and I felt I could still fix it. Instead, it turned to be a cycle, and the more I tried and tried, I was in the same situation again and again. On my own, I finally figured out what I had to do. I literally talked to myself and told myself, "Hey, she has gone the furthest way possible to make this be so real. She is in her own very way informing you of her life's memories, tragedies, and challenging times, although at the same time, she is escaping from two heavy chains that were holding her back, from realizing her true desires of life, as well as her short-term and long-term goals." And yes, here it is, a message from a mother's heart.

Ana Lydia Chavez

A Message From A Mother's Heart

The Autobiography of A Mexican Americanized Woman

Austin Macauley Publishers™
LONDON • CAMBRIDGE • NEW YORK • SHARJAH

Copyright © Ana Lydia Chavez 2023

All rights reserved. No part of this publication may be reproduced, distributed, or transmitted in any form or by any means, including photocopying, recording, or other electronic or mechanical methods, without the prior written permission of the publisher, except in the case of brief quotations embodied in critical reviews and certain other non-commercial uses permitted by copyright law. For permission requests, write to the publisher.

Any person who commits any unauthorized act in relation to this publication may be liable to criminal prosecution and civil claims for damages.

All of the events in this memoir are true to the best of author's memory. The views expressed in this memoir are solely those of the author.

Ordering Information
Quantity sales: Special discounts are available on quantity purchases by corporations, associations, and others. For details, contact the publisher at the address below.

Publisher's Cataloging-in-Publication data
Chavez, Ana Lydia
A Message from a Mother's Heart

ISBN 9781645366591 (Paperback)
ISBN 9781647509354 (Hardback)
ISBN 9781647509361 (ePub e-book)
ISBN 9781647509491 (Audiobook)

Library of Congress Control Number: 2023908134

www.austinmacauley.com/us

First Published 2023
Austin Macauley Publishers LLC
40 Wall Street, 33rd Floor, Suite 3302
New York, NY 10005
USA

mail-usa@austinmacauley.com
+1 (646) 5125767

I would like to acknowledge Ms. Edna Cline, she is a woman I met when assisting her to sell her condo. I learned she was an English Major, she graduated from Fresno State, and I asked her to look at my writing I had almost completed. She was very helpful. She gave me ideas on how to make my script more interesting and commented that it felt to her that my book was similar to a Mexican Novela. Thank you, Edna.

Table of Contents

Prologue	**13**
Introduction	**16**
Part I: Finding My Path	**21**
My Daughters, Nieces, and Nephew	29
A Little Menace	42
All About Moving to America	64
Surpresa!	70
Life Starts in America	73
Words Hurt More	76
Oh, Dios Mio! What Is This?	80
Part II	**81**
My Dreams; De Nina a Mujer (From Child to Woman)	83
First Time for Everything	110
My Awakening	147

Prologue

When I was a young girl, I dreamed of becoming famous. All I ever wanted then was to sing, dance, act, or be someone to be known. Maybe, that's what many little girls dream of at one time in their childhood lives. Well, some young girls are really born to sing, dance, and be movie stars or models. I, for a fact, was not born to do any of the ladders, but I enjoyed dreaming it. It gave me life. The truth of it all is that it felt great to dream. Ever since I was a little thing, I fantasized about the stars, the moon, and the sun. I never knew how big the world really was from where I lived; I just knew that someday I was going to do something, something big, I just did not know what.

As a young adult, those dreams sort of faded. However, a new one suddenly appeared. I wanted to be a nurse. For a long time, I felt so close to becoming a nurse; then, I found out after I became a certified nursing assistant that becoming a nursing assistant was just the beginning. I was told that I needed to go to college, then take more and more classes to become a registered nurse. Right then, I knew that being a nurse was a long way away. My dreams were crushed because I had no clue how to get into college, and being an immigrant, there was no chance. That dream, again crushed. So, I settled by staying as a certified nursing assistant and working at a convalescent hospital. These facilities or places are known today as Assisted Living or Retirement Centers. I guess I gave up too soon on my dreams. If I really wanted it, I should have stuck with it and made it mine. "Maybe it was not meant to be." That's how I used to think; that was the safest way to comfort myself. How wrong and foolish I always was. I went my whole childhood and young adult life by just settling for less, accepting just the way things were, never asking questions, never did I dare to critically think or even think outside the box, wow!

The last thing I want to do is make excuses for my life, as far as why I didn't go to college, why I didn't follow my dreams and why I was such a mess! I can't blame anyone else but myself. I accepted what has happened in my life. I actually feel very lucky that I survived it all. I feel that God's hand and Mama's prayers have been over my life. After having gone through it all in my life, I do have some regrets but have learned to embrace those. That's all part of life; I have learned from my failures. If you think about it, if we go through life not accepting our failures, we never learn. I feel I've learned and still am learning. We never stop learning and should never stop trying. Maybe some of you are thinking, "Sure, sounds way too easy." I know it is not so easy. We are humans, and nobody is perfect. It's okay to make mistakes, but never stop trying and never quit on yourself. Someday, you'll get it right. Remember to always surround yourself with people who love you and want to see you succeed. But don't be stubborn, like the way I was. Really! Pay attention, learn to listen with your heart, and look to receive positive advice from your parents, a mentor, like your teacher, a minister, or someone that really cares for your wellbeing, just believe that you are a wonderful person no matter what happened in the past, if you are ready to change, you will make it in life.

Throughout my life, God sent me amazing people; they all kept me going. I can easily count on those people, and thinking back now, how each individually treated me, I know what they saw in me. My head was so scrambled that I couldn't see what they were seeing in me and how they were really trying to help me. Maybe I had trust issues, low self-esteem, no confidence, helplessness, or any other issues going on that prohibited me from growing as a person and becoming successful in my studies to one day reach my highest potentials. That's what I mean when I say never quit on yourself, keep trying and never give up.

Introduction

Dear Reader,

My family and I have lived in California for the past forty-two years. This 4th of July 2020 will be year number forty-three since we migrated from Mexico. I have remembered back all those years; I'm glad to say that our family has done well; we can't complain. We, the children, and my parents worked hard. We suffered through poverty, but I must be thankful, after all the sacrifices, trials, and tribulations we've experienced, we had enough of what was needed to survive.

Our parents knew exactly what they were doing by teaching us to work and pay for our own clothes; whenever we wanted something new, Papa would say, "I will take you children out this weekend *a Piscar Chiles* (to pick chilies)." This would happen at least every weekend, and of course, on summer breaks, we worked every day. That is, if there were no scheduled *Migra* (border patrol) raids Papa and Mama would listen for over the AM radio, if there were none announced by El Senor Tirado, a well-known advocate for immigrants and disc-jockey during the 1970s, then it was set, we went to work. And when there were, that's when our parents would say, "No, not today the border patrol is active." My brothers, sister, and I would play around and say, "Good, we want the '*Migra*' to take us back to San Luis." Our parents, of course, would get mad because that was exactly what they were avoiding. They were just doing their best to show us how to survive and stay away from troubles. Those were difficult times, but they were good survival tactics that our parents were teaching us. I for sure didn't see it that way; I don't know if the rest of my siblings did see it that way. Until now, and when I decided to change my path, I could see why my parents did what they did, why we were brought to another country, here to the U.S.A., why we left our home, family, and friends.

Today, when things get tough in my life, I think back to how as a family, we survived, how we coped with all of our difficulties, the sacrifices, and humiliations we each went throughout whether it was in school, places we went, or our parents in their work environment. We only know because we lived it, and we survived it. Our parents were very strong, and they were doing just that, teaching us how to be strong, too.

Now that I'm a parent, I realize a parent's job is the most difficult thing to do. It involves more than just loving and caring for them. It is to teach them responsibilities, good morals, be respectful, and to be well mannered too. It was up to me to teach my children that things aren't just handed over when they ask, "Give me" should be more like, "Mom, what can I help you with around the house?" It was up to me to teach them to be respectful toward others and to have respect for themselves too.

But who am I kidding? I am not even sure if I've done a good job as a parent. Because I can truly admit that there were times during my life's crisis as a mother, I failed my lovely children. What I am sure and believe, that we are all good people, it's just, sometimes we lose our path and go the wrong direction, like lost little lambs. That is why I felt obligated to share my thoughts and feelings about the real me. Actually, I have been writing this for the past six years, and I have gone over and over one-thousand times. And it doesn't fail; every time I read it, I get anxious. Because I cannot get over the fear of who I was. I honestly don't know how I made it this far in life. I lacked everything; confidence, brains, creativity, and intelligence. (Oh, I already said brains!) So, you get the picture. Although, one special thing that I did not lack was my family. And it didn't matter how dysfunctional we were then, and we are now. They all have helped me to survive this crazy and insane life I've lived. We still help one another. Also, if you just keep trying, you'll get where you want to be.

For some people, it is easy to accomplish their goals and make their dreams come true with little or no effort. That's because that's who they are, they are gifted, and that's alright. And remember, there are a few of them who are born on a silver platter, and even then, they have to learn to cope; even for those fortunate individuals, there are struggles. I am so happy for those individuals. For me, things just haven't been that easy. As an adult, I always asked myself, "Why can't I catch a break?" Have you felt that way before? Maybe you have, maybe you haven't. I don't know. But what I do know is that I have learned from my failures, which have been many.

I feel that I changed my direction from the wrong path to the better one, not only for me but for my children and family. I know that by being shy and staying quiet, I can't help anyone. So I took the initiative to express myself, even if it's a handful of people or just one person, who read this book, just the thought of helping someone, it brings me joy and hope to keep succeeding in making a difference.

So, please you, yes you! Take this leap of faith like I did, when finally, I trusted in myself to do what I always wanted to do. I went back to school and, this time, didn't quit. So, trust in yourself, you'll see, wonderful things can happen. The universe aligns perfectly when you are ready to believe and feel inspired to find the path that leads you to a successful life.

Part I
Finding My Path

In January 2009, right after President Barack Obama was inaugurated, officially, as the new president of the United States. I decided to take a leap of faith. I returned to school, it had been over twenty-five years since I had graduated from high school, yet I was determined to do it. It was not easy at first, but like everything else, it was a matter of getting used to. I was motivated by his campaign speeches about education. Even though it meant for me to start from the bottom. My level of education was equivalent to 7th or 8th grade. Math, reading, and writing all needed to be improved. That was not the worst of it; the worse was being in a classroom full of eighteen and twenty-year-old students, students that knew more than me. I was so embarrassed, and I had not picked up a textbook in so long. The way teachers and students communicated was strange to me. The language was the same; just the topics were things I had not heard of or did not remember hearing when I was in high school. It was since then the last time I spoke to a teacher, in 1986. That's when I found out it was no longer the 1980s when my government teacher in high school would compare me to an Italian movie star. This was now the 21st century, and, in college. I was just an illiterate forty-year-old student mom. Oh yeah! First few weeks, I almost gave up. It felt awful! It was as if I was back in first grade, except in this large woman's body. At first, I was so eager, so excited to be there and learn, but my brain was no longer the brain of a first-grader, like a sponge. It was the opposite, the non-absorbing type. In just about every class, the lectures were going over my head; I didn't know the words, and what the heck were they talking about? It was just way too complicated. I felt it was much too overwhelming. I wanted to do the thing I knew most how to do when things were just not going well, quit. Except, this time around, in my life, there was someone who helped me stay true to myself. My boyfriend, which I will talk about in the last chapter of this book. I owe it to him, for the most part, for helping me get through the toughest part of college. He helped me not to quit. Instead, he helped me to learn, listen and focus. And I started to speak up, thank God! My brain started to change and learn some. I was less scared by the second semester. And after one year in college, I had managed to make the dean's list, and that was not all, on the following year, again. My level of confidence was high, and very much motivated. So, I bet you are asking, "How did she do it?" I did it by asking questions, speaking up to professors, teachers, counselors, my peers, getting help, help, and more help. Something I never did before. I would get home from class; I would go over my notes, listen to recorded lectures, reading the assigned text chapters, re-read, and study, study, study. I was one of those individuals that it did not matter; if I was in class every day, I had to study in order for it to stick. Oh! Yes, I forgot to mention, I did not cut any classes. It did not matter what was going on in my adult life; I had to be responsible. I learned to communicate with my brain. It sounds weird, but it works;

there were times my old brain wanted to do it one way when knowing well it was not that way. I played tricks with it until I found what would work; it's as if I re-programed it; achieved it by learning other methods. Let me tell you; nothing is easy, that is for sure. I always admired all those young, vibrant, and more intellectual peers than me; I would say, "Oh my, If I only had that brain." I started to sound like the Wizard of Oz's character, Scare Crow, but I learned to accept myself as to who I was and being grateful to God for what he had given me. It was all in my head, just like the Lion, another character in the Wizard of Oz, I thought I had no courage, but I always had it in me.

On one occasion, I was taking a summer course, computer class, as a matter of fact, one of those required courses. There were two young men, intelligent, those overachievers in the area of technology. The instructor, as an initial assignment, asked us to share the reason (s) for taking the course? Each of us had to respond on the blackboard and then respond to two classmate's comments. I had very little knowledge of computers and software; I knew the very basic "Log on" and "Log off," type, and search the browser. Well, I made it a point to read the comments of these two young overachievers; you can tell just by reading their comments that they were very smart. I had to pass this class; there was no way that I was going to sacrifice my whole summer and flunk the course. So, I wrote down their names in my writing journal and wrote this, "My name is Ana Lydia Chavez, the reason why I am taking this course 'Computer 15' is because it is a requirement and even though I know quite a bit about computers, software and the hard drives, I would love to learn more and also because I love technology." At the end of that, I wrote the names of the two young men and wrote, "I want to be just like them" (I would do this for every subject, math, biology, chem class, you name it). The very first week, I read the textbook and studied very hard for my first test and pop quiz. I had great grades, yes, the class did get harder as the weeks passed, but I stuck to it. The whole course was only six weeks, so you can imagine the instructor was going super fast. I must admit I did pass the class; I believe it was a C grade, I know! But I didn't flunk.

I knew there were bumps in the road that caused me concussions; I lost the path, and getting back up was the hardest, but once the oxygen reached my brain and my blood flowed properly, I found the right path finally saw the yellow brick road. The reason I call it the yellow brick road is that a few years, to be exact, in May 2015, I graduated from a CSU, Fresno State. I made it! Yes, I am very proud to have accomplished this as I am the second in my family to have graduated from a college or university.

My degree is not as a nurse, as that was my dream; I sort of left that in the past. Instead, I chose to be a criminologist with an emphasis on victims of crime or an advocate for victims. I feel that is not too far from being a nurse; in a way is very similar, as in both professions is about healing. That is exactly what happened to me as I transformed myself into this career. In the next chapters, I will talk to you about my life and different stories throughout my life, as a sexually abused child, suffering a traumatic culture shock, being bullied at school, and finding one of my siblings dead after he committed suicide. All of these traumas I suffered as a child and throughout my teenage years. And all of that was a direct reflection in my adult years. The traumas that I never healed from, with both an injured heart and mind. I had old wounds that repeatedly dug deeper and deeper.

I don't know when I lost faith in myself because I know at one time I had faith, but along the way, that faith was covered with fear and masked with the traumas, with the chaos that was living inside of me. For a long time, I stopped dreaming. It took a while before the confidence in me to return and do what I was brought to this land to do. Those traumatized moments were not easy to forget when you go through life with those memory triggers that come back and haunt you, like ghosts in one's head that become so strong that they take control of you. "Oh yes, they tested me, but I'm now in control." Yes, this was something I did not know back then. The triggers in my mind were emotions that I was not recognizing. Although, I never recognized what was going on in my head. Like why was I such a failure in relationships? Why would I always pick the wrong guys? I would have never known until I had a talk with myself. I now know what those memory triggers mean, there are merely bad nightmares, and they were there all the time, and I was afraid and was always in search of someone or something to mask the pain. But this was not until later in my life that I learned what a victimized individual goes through or a person in trauma. My studies helped me to understand how to deal with such things. But before that, I had no idea, except to listen to God's messages and follow his path. I had to stop listening to my voice because, obviously, I was headed for destruction.

Unfortunate things happen to people, and it can make you feel like if a tidal wave is on you and no matter how fast you swim to avoid it, you cannot escape it, the more you want to avoid it; getting out of the way from it, so that you do not drown, is impossible because it is bigger than what you can handle. It covers you completely, unable to breathe, and its strong, powerful arms push you around like a rag doll. Well, until finally, you get just enough power to breathe again, power to get strength and take those strong arms off you and stand up and step on that wave and just walk right above it, until your feet step on firm sand and firmly stand on both feet without stumbling; and suddenly your whole being is completely alive. I felt this way always as a child, as a teen, young adult, and even during the two times I was married and had my two daughters. I did not understand what was happening to me; I thought I was crazy; I felt so misunderstood. It was frustrating; it was very demoralizing. I don't think I was trying to get attention or wanted people to feel sorry for me. I just kept trying and fall and get back up. Once I learned what really happened and accepted it, I was free.

My goals are to help society, those who have lost their path, those who have stopped dreaming, and those who thought they had no purpose in life. They need to know that it is really "Never" too late. We all have a special niche; we all are good at something. For some people, it is easier than others to find it. For others, like me, it can take almost half their lifetime. The main ingredient is we just need to have faith in ourselves and conquer those fears that are stopping us from discovering them. Once you do, you can't help feeling so relieved and extremely happy to be so alive.

My Daughters, Nieces, andNephew

Then came the day my daughters, nieces, and nephew became teenagers and started asking to go out. I began to panic. Just thinking back to my years as an adolescent, it was driving me crazy. I was not allowing my oldest daughter, Victoria, to have friends, go out, and have a boyfriend. That was out of the question.

When I finally had a talk with my daughter, she said to me, "Mom, I'm a good girl; I listen to you and know that you do not want me to get pregnant nor use drugs." Victoria is a very sweet but gullible young adult. She is very smart and has no space for hate in her heart. She was always very responsible as a daughter, and as a student, I think a bit too much because there were many times that she worried when I was running late to drop her off at the bus stop or to school. Throughout Victoria's elementary and junior high years, she maintained a 4.0-grade point average and was so dedicated to every sport. Her favorite was soccer, but she quit way too soon. She could have been great in all sports if she was not so hard on herself. Unlike me, she has always been a fast learner; she is very smart and has grown up to be a responsible adult.

That is exactly why I was relieved and blessed to hear those words come from her heart to her mouth. I thought I was doing my job as a mother having the talk that every mother should have with her daughter. But I realized that I really had not. Because what I wanted to share with my daughter was why I was concerned. It was not that I did not trust her nor that I did not want her to go out and have fun. I was just afraid she would make the same mistakes I did when I was young.

By the time Victoria turned eighteen, her sister, Laura, my youngest, was fourteen years old. One night, they were having a sister-to-sister talk in their bedroom. When I peaked in to see what they were doing, they asked me to come in; they said, "Mom, we have something to ask you."

I said, "What? What is it?" I was a bit embarrassed even though these two innocent children came from me; I knew what they were talking about. I saw it in their inquiring eyes and shy smiles. They finally asked me, as they saw my irritation and stress level rise, "Mom, at what age you lost your virginity?"

My face was red like a hot tamale! The next words out of my mouth were, "Why, why are you asking me this?"

They said they were curious.

I did not answer their question. I simply said, "I will talk to you about this when I'm ready." I asked them if they were still virgins? They both answered, "Yes." Their innocent smiles and wondering minds convinced me to believe in them. I then reminded them that the most precious thing a girl has, was her innocence, and I was totally aware that times had changed from when girls went to the altar as virgins. I just wanted them to make wise choices as to whom they gave themselves. I also told them that whenever they felt it was time to take that huge step, I would like to know first so we could talk about different means to prevent pregnancy and other types of problems that come along with being sexually active. I told them much rather that they would concentrate on their studies than having a boyfriend and thinking about sex. For me, having this conversation with my little ones was comforting to my heart because my sister and I did not have this mother-daughter talk with ours, which might have cleared up a lot of our questions and curiosities.

Victoria shared to me that most of her friends had boyfriends and some were already sexually involved, and she felt a bit under pressure. Yes. I understood her exactly since I experienced the very same thing when I was in school. I just did not know how to tell Mama and make her understand what I felt because she worked every day and seemed to be tired or in a bad mood with Papa. But this was not going to be the case with my children; I use to think.

That day was the most wonderful day of my motherhood. I felt I had to come clean with these kiddies. I had an "Aha" moment, as Oprah says. So, I decided to write down all my moments as a teenager, the age I had my first boyfriend, and when I lost my virginity. I just could not face my daughters since I felt I was bad when I was young. So, I wrote these notes to share with them that I had rushed my years as a young teen. I made some bad decisions. However, I also made it clear to them that I did not regret having either one of them in my life. Things always worked out for the best. Victoria and Laura are the two greatest things that came out of my wild and crazy years.

Laura is my youngest, and just like all siblings, she is very different than her sister. Their only similarity is that they are from the same mother, and both have beautiful hearts. Although, Laura reminds me a bit more of myself. I noticed things in her as a child, teen, and now in her twenties; she was always the center of attention, so fascinated with being a model, dancing, and just doing what she loves and enjoys, unlike me she is doing and enjoying it. I remember one time she was five years old; I told her not to overeat because she was always getting an upset stomach. She looked up and said, "I want to look like you, Mommy."

After Laura was born, I could never get my figure back. I tried to lose weight, worked out, diets, and the "Baby fat" never fell off me. But the day Laura said that to me, I tried even harder for her to see how I wanted to lose weight and eat healthier, and thanks to her Auntie Annie, she maintained very active with sports and dance.

After they read my handwritten in blue ink confessions, my daughters were not so surprised. They said they kind of thought that because Grandma once told them that I was wild and that I was a big *volada (flirt)*. So that is when I figured out that my girls were way much smarter than me. When I told them that was the reason I was overprotective with them, they both said, "Mom, we are not as bad as you were!" Oh, my lord! I thought. They were right. At that moment, I transformed into a totally different mom. It was not easy to speak with my children about sex. As in Mexican culture sex, it's seen as a stigma; you don't mention how a man and a woman come together to experience such things. There is no way, my daughters helped me to have such conversations, no it was not easy, but at least when the time came, when they were ready to become sexually active, it was when both were adults and ready to accept the responsibilities that come with such decisions. That's what I thought. Really?! How wrong I was.

When my oldest came to me, I was crushed. I didn't know what to do. I can recall that same week, I had a math final, and I could not concentrate, as math is my worst subject. And I could not even talk to my mother because I would hear it from her, I could picture the smirk on her face and her telling me, "Now, you know what I went through with you." Shoot!

So, for the next few days, I was sort of quiet and kept to myself; I would go online and search for articles about how other mothers deal with their daughters having sex. I even took a quiz on Oprah's website and found out that I needed certain skills to speak with my daughters about sex. Suddenly, I came across a blog titled, "I'm not as bad as you were, Mom."

Wow! That hit a nerve. This was the second time I became aware of that. The article was written by Gabrielle Gary and Kathy Lette, also the authors of Puberty Blues. After I read their article, I felt much better about myself and completely embraced my daughter's decision. By going through that experience with my oldest daughter, I hoped to do better with the youngest, and yes, it was a little better, but it really is never easy. With each daughter or son is, the situation is completely different. The only thing that matters is for a parent to be there, ready to help their son or daughter, and hope for them to embrace your advice.

As far as my lovely nieces go, I'm a very proud auntie; my lovely sister Angela has blessed me with three beautiful nieces. They are all completely different, Krystel is her first born, a delicate and petite young girl; she did not inherit her tia's traits of being a flirt because I did not see her date a boy until her Prom. I admire her drive to be a healthy eater and so in control of her "Persona." I'm proud, so proud of Krystel Eve it is a pleasure being her tia (aunt). I'm very sure she will shine in whatever she puts her mind to achieve her goals and desires.

Krystel came into this world in a very challenging way. Her desire to live was the most amazing thing I had ever seen in my life. I was with my sister in the delivery room; as her coach, at eighteen, I had no idea how a child was to look when being born. I thought as a nursing assistant, I had seen it all, but I was wrong. Krystel's delivery had been prolonged because her mother's body was quite not ready. When she finally was born, the doctor and nurse saw something I did not, Krystel's stomach had an opening on the area of her belly button, and her large intestines were literally out. I did not want to panic nor panic my sister, but I could not help feeling worried for this new baby girl and her mother, my sister. The doctor asked me to cut the cord, but it happened so fast, and then before her mom, Angela, could cuddle her, Krystel was rushed to Valley Children's Hospital. Thirty-one years have gone by, but I feel like it was yesterday.

I can still remember the nurse asking Angela if she had a name picked out for her. I thought to myself, "Wow! Really! What is her name going to be?" My sister responded right away, "Her name is Krystel Eve." when I heard that, I was amazed to hear her response so calmly, despite all that was happening. The nurse even told her, "Wow, that is a beautiful name," my sister said, "Yes, that is the name of one of the characters in the show Dynasty. Angela, my sister, spent her maternity leave watching Dynasty and The Dallas Show, and that is how she picked my niece's name."

The next day as soon as my sister was released from the hospital, she rushed to Valley Children's Hospital. The building was located at the avenues of Shields and Millbrook, which, currently, is now known as Heritage Center. Currently, The Children's Hospital is just off of Highway 41, in the city of Madera. Well, back then, it was in Fresno, and Angela drove every day to be near her newborn baby girl and did not want to move from her side. "A mother's love for her child is difficult to explain; it's an instinct, no matter how far a mother is away from its child, she will always feel its child's pain and worries." My sister did not know if her child would make it, but she prayed to God every day for her child to get healthy; she and only the physicians, nurses, and the parents could be in the room where Krystel was kept. The next few days after born, my sister asked me if it was okay for me to be my niece's Godmother; as a Catholic, the priest advised Angela to honor her Christianity beliefs and to be prepared in case God called her to leave us. Krystel was baptized while in the hospital. I was not present; only the priest, her mom, and dad were.

Three whole months went by until the day came, Krystel's homecoming. She was finally to enjoy the beautiful nursery that her mother had prepared for her a few months prior to her birth. It was wonderful to finally see her enjoy it and for us to see her home. It was such a beautiful feeling having a baby in the family since we were all full-grown; we did not know what it felt like to have a little one cry, giggle and poop. Krystel brought joy to all of us. Mama and Papa were now *abuelitos* (grandparents), and Krystel took advantage of that attention; she was spoiled, she was a princess, and she knew it.

Until, the next baby girl came around, my first, Victoria. Although that really did not bother Krystel very much, she enjoyed her new cousin and had no problem sharing her space. It was not until her sister Missy was born that is when she felt threatened.

Actually, everything sort of changed when Missy was born; she was strong and wanted things her way and only her way. She cried at night all the time and wanted to be rocked to sleep all night long. Missy was so white, white as Snow White, and had reddish hair like Ariel from The Little Mermaid. She grew up to be full of life and really did not give a rats-ass who she ran over. Her dad would comment whenever she got in trouble around the house; that's just how he imagined her to be; he would call her a destroyer and say, "Esa es mi hija" (that's my daughter).

Missy's Papa loved her dearly. I am not able to share much about him because he and my sister were together for a very short term. All I can say that when Missy was about four years of age, one day, he left the house and never returned. He and my sister did not agree on things of life. His eyes never saw his ginger-haired girl ever again. Missy has never seen the way her father enjoyed seeing her so full of life and joy. His eyes resemble her, and there is no doubt that wherever he is, he is thinking of her. Some people say he's no longer alive, and some say he is. I say dead or alive he is around her to make sure she will always be just great.

The last time Missy saw her dad was the summer I was expecting Laura, the summer of 1994. First, before jumping into Laura's story, I want to share the story of when I took the girls to Disneyland.

It was right before the girls, Missy and Victoria, turned three; Krystel was turning seven. It would be the first time they would see all the Disney characters live. The whole day was full of fun and adventure. Until the parade on the main street was over, both girls, Missy and Victoria, were in strollers, and Krystel was standing next to me watching when Missy jumped out from the stroller and walked away with the people as the parade ended; she moved away with the crowd toward the exit. I turned around to gather the girls, when suddenly I realized one was missing, of course, Missy! I instantly panicked like a "*Loca*" I was pushing away through the crowds of people screaming her name loudly, "Missy! Missy! Missy!" But all I got was the people's attention; some people asked me what was wrong? Others simply ignored me and continued with their lives. I would remember to return to the other two girls in between my misery and tell them not to move and to wait for John (John is the father of Laura, who, of course, was not yet born at the time). I finally bumped into John, he and I had just moved in together, and this was our first trip out of town. He had just stepped away before the parade had finished purchasing some souvenirs for his mom and dad. He finds me a mess, and I do not know whether to cry or scream or just do both at the same time. He screamed at me and said, "Calm down! Which way did she go?" he asked; I pointed toward the exit. I was really not too sure; I did not even see her get out of the stroller. How was I to know where she went. I suddenly had a hunch not to move away from that spot, I felt her near, and I was not about to call my sister with the awful news. John set out to look for her, and I stayed in the same spot waiting for Missy's return while I held on to Krystel and Victoria with my dear life.

I could not stop turning in all the directions of the park; at that moment, I felt like a predator as if I had X-ray vision until in one of my quick looks, I saw a small little girl walking next to two Disney attendants; Missy was like if nothing had happened, she was as happy as can be admiring the small shop stores and caressing on the windows as if she was window shopping. I ran and grabbed her; she smiled at me and said, "Nina!" The employees asked me if she was mine; I said yes; they said they saw her wandering by the exit, they were on their way to take her to the headquarters. Oh, Lord!

Afterward, John returned; he was still in a panic and was eager to end our visit to the fantasy land, but not with a smile. Well, I should say he was relieved. That night, back at the Hotel, John had no more self-control; he had refrained from an alcoholic beverage all day and the night before. But not after that, hell no! he fell off the wagon sort of speak.

John had a drinking problem; I never knew how bad it was or how an alcoholic behaved. I never was around people who drank as John did. On this Disneyland trip, especially after the fright of losing a child that was not ours. Let's just say the stress level was off the charts. John began to become very grouchy with the girls; Missy was crying out of control, the girls and I were exhausted. I noticed his short temper and how he was being anointed with the girls, which is why I told him he needed to calm down. He left the room and did not return until much later until the girls were asleep; I fell to sleep too. But before that, the girls had baths, we ate dinner, and off to bed, we went. John, on the other hand, did not; he stayed up drinking. The next morning, when I got out of bed, I discovered my feet stepping and jumping over many miniature liquors bottles. I did not know what had happened. I did not know where all these bottles came from. I looked over where John was, and the bottles trailed to his whereabouts. That morning the girls and I got ready for breakfast, and we all got ready to drive back to Fresno.

Today, Missy continues to wander off to Disneyland, but she is now twenty-nine years old. I'm happy she returned to us that day in Disneyland, safe and sound. She always seemed to live her life free of worries, as we should, because it does not make any sense worrying about things that we do not know how they are going to turnout, or that out of our control.

Missy is a strong, smart, and beautiful young lady. She, like Krystel, felt that she would be the center of attention for a long time until I brought Laura to the addition. Let's just say Laura rocked things a bit too much for them after she started to walk, talk and want it her way, only her way.

Everything was okay; the three girls were having the time of their lives; my sister and I went places together with them and did daily activities with them, too. Well, Laura broke the perfect bond. It was hard for Victoria, I know, and harder for the other two girls, Krystel and Missy. Because Laura was spoiled with two families, Laura was the lucky one to have two sets of grandparents, aunts, and uncles, and more cousins; she was the one that opened Christmas presents throughout the day and the next day too. Although it was pretty challenging keeping the peace between them, Victoria always did her best in standing up for her little sister, and it would bring a bit of turmoil between her and Krystel. For some reason, Victoria and Krystel would understand and get along better than the other two. All I can say when they played with their Barbies, it was never a dull moment. Laura would make their lives difficult. Laura always wanted things her way, and let's just say that Krystel would lose her patience with Laura and would immediately stop playing. Laura always had her way of turning stories around and would always end up okay out the whole ordeal.

Soon after, Laura started preschool and seemed to get along better with the rest of the girls because she begins to interact with children of her same age. Laura's auntie, Annie, started her on tee-ball and has kept her busy since from soccer to basketball, soccer, softball, and hip hop dance. But before all that, my lovely sweet Emma was born on February 10, 2000.

Emma is my sister's youngest; she is fifteen years apart from Krystel and nine years apart from her Missy. This makes Emma the baby from the family. She is *guera* (blond) with green eyes just like "*Mama*." Interestingly, out of all the granddaughters, she, Emma, is the only one that is very similar to Mama's genotype. Well, Victoria's eyes came close; they are hazel in color.

Whenever I see Emma, I picture Mama born all over again. I saw a picture of Mama when she was young, like Emma's age now, 20 years old, and they resemble each other very much. Except that Emma will grow to be a very tall young woman and Mama, well, she stopped growing a long time ago and seems like the older she gets, she loses inches. Emma is very artistic; she is quiet but is always thinking, and when she speaks, is to tell a joke, she loves to draw. Emma seems to have all the characteristics of all of us; it is like she is all of us in one.

What I mean by that is that she looks like Mom, acts like me, and has her mom's elegant style, and looks very high class. She loves music like her sisters and is very smart like them too. Emma is tall like I was at her age, and let's just say physically, she is well portioned just like I was on the chest. She shares with me that her sisters and my daughters make fun of her. I tell her, "Do not pay any attention, be proud of who you are and what God gave you; they are just jealous." I told her that I went through that too, and right now, she may not understand, but she should be proud of the body God and her parents gave her. It is shameful that people make fun of people because if you think about it, we are all very similar to one another. We are humans from the same planet.

Zeke Chavez Moreno is my only nephew. He is my youngest brother's son, my only brother, I should say. Zeke grew up not as close to the family as the rest of my nieces but always was around to see him grow. Currently, now that he is in his early twenties, the family is closer to him, and we are all very proud of him; he is following his dad's steps as far as in a business mentality aspect. Zeke is very intelligent and, most of all, respectful, loving, and caring toward his mother, who raised him as a single mom. We all owe his mother much respect and gratitude for keeping him near us despite the fall-out relationship with her and my brother. Thank You! Zeke's Mom. You know who you are.

A Little Menace

Late at night during a summer storm on August 3, 1967, I was born in a medium-sized clinic in the village of Sonora, Mexico. The proud parents were a thirty-two-year-old farm worker and his lovely twenty-four-year-old wife. Mama was a homemaker who also cared for my three siblings, Sergio, six, Angela, four, and Luis Fernando, two years old. Our family lived in a valley about a one-hour drive from the main city of San Luis Rio Colorado, Sonora, Mexico.

My father a handsome man. He is presently eighty-five years old, but he still has traces of how nice-looking he once was. Papa was the oldest of eight children; their family was very poor. My father was born in Amacueca, Jalisco, Mexico, whose mother died when my father was ten. Papa had to grow up really quickly; he began to work and cared for his younger siblings. His father was an alcoholic and was very abusive toward them, too. Papa moved away from his hometown, along with him came two of his younger brothers. Their plans were to cross to the United States and work as Braceros, which they did enroll and worked for a few years, and send money to support their younger sisters. They did as they planned. The two brothers did not return to their hometown. Later, Dad, before he married Mama, he ended up working in the valley where Mama lived. By that time, father was twenty-four, they settled in *La Esperanza Village*, where he and Mama met and got married.

Mama was a beautiful young woman with green eyes and the whitest skin a Mexican can have due to the mixture of Spanish blood. She was born in the same place I was. She was one of the seven children of two farm owners in the valley. Her parents were one of the first families to arrive in this small colony called *La Esperanza*, meaning hope in English. My grandparents became owners of agricultural land and survived by working their land, planting cotton, wheat and alfalfa. When Mama met Papa, she was seventeen, soon after they eloped.

When I was young, I did not get to meet my mama's father nor my papa's parents. I was fortunate to have one grandmother, Mama's Mama. She preferred for us to call her "Mama Nita" because she did not want to be called *Abuelita* (grandma). I guess it was because she was so young when her husband died and then became responsible for the *rancho* (farm); she had no time to be the loving mother-grandma style. According to my mother, she says she remembers very little of her father. He was killed by two *banditos* (Bad Hombres), who posed as laborers, but he soon found out they were stealing from him.

I do not remember how old I was when we moved away from *La Esperanza*. All my cousins, when we were younger, referred to it as '*El Rancho*'. Most of my mother's siblings and their families lived there. But our grandmother and her oldest son moved away with his family to the nearest town, San Luis Rio, Colorado. I'm not sure what year Mama and Papa moved to the city of San Luis Rios, Colorado.

However, just from what my memory recalls, it was a couple of years after my little youngest brother was born. So, that would have made me four years old because we are about two years apart.

Mama and Papa rented a home from Tio Roberto, Mama Anita's youngest brother. Since he and his family lived in Fresno, California, he had no personal use for the home, plus it is never good to leave a house alone in Mexico. From time to time, I saw Tio Roberto at Mama Nita's house. Tio Alberto and Mama Nita were stepbrother and sister, but I never knew the relationship between them until we came to live here. I did not even know; we were living in his house and that my parents paid him rent. When you are young, these concerns do not come to mind. Nevertheless, the house was like our home. The house was located between the streets of *La Libertad y Carranza*, nowadays Mama's brother lives in it; he bought it from Tio Alberto a few years after we had already moved to the United States.

The house had three large bedrooms, a large kitchen, and one huge living room. You can say it was a living room, although we did not own a living room set. So, we used it as a bedroom. The bathroom was outside (outhouse), and we showered in a small room that had a drain connected to the wall to send the water outside.

My mama would heat water on the gas stove early in the morning for us to shower since the house did not have a bathroom nor shower. When it was time for our shower, she would mix some of the hot water to cold water in a big *bandeja* (tin container). We then had warm water and poured it over our heads and bodies with an *olla* (metal pot). I didn't like when mom bathed us because she would hurry up and when she poured the water over our head, it felt as if we were drowning. One thing is for sure, we were poor but always very well-groomed.

The property's lot size was huge. I remember we even had two pigs, one goat, and some chickens. We used to feed the pigs and often had to run after one of them, because it always got away.

I'm pretty sure Mama prepared a lot of *caldos de pollo* (chicken noodle soups) for us with the chickens we had because there would be less and less until all of them were gone. The pigs and the goats were also gone after a while. There were times that our parents did not have money, mom did not work since she took care of us, and dad, when he was not working in the United States, would stay in Mexico and work in nightclubs selling cigarettes. There were many mouths to feed, and I am sure there were many desperate times. Difficult and hard times that only Papa and Mama knew.

The neighbors were all very friendly, except I can't say the same for the lady that lived on the left of our house. Mama called her '*la bruja del 71*', that name refers to a character from a famous comedy Mexican show, El Chavo Del Ocho, because she was mean to her children, a boy, and a girl, as well as her husband. She was not a friendly person to the rest of the neighbors. Even though my mama did not care for her, she still worked for her by ironing, sewing, and knitting clothes. I'm sure for minimum wages. But I know it helped Mama buy milk, eggs, and bread to feed her five children, especially when Papa was not sending money from the U.S.A.

My mama was always telling us, my brothers, sister, and me, not to go inside their home or take anything from them. Mama wanted the least communication possible, even though they gave Mama work for us to survive.

Now, I know why she said it. A mother never wants anything bad to happen to her children.

I was usually the one getting into trouble since I can remember; I was the one not listening to Mama. I would always do the complete opposite. I'm sure you have heard of the 'terrible twos'. Well, in my case, those 'terrible twos' hung around for a longer period. For me, it was nothing but trouble. One of the memories I have of those occasions was when my mother found me on top of a big tree that was to the left of the front of our house, near '*The bruja*'s' house. I was eating Hershey chocolate bar, a bag of them was there when I got there. And, the next thing I know, Lidia was in chocolate heaven. (Maybe that's why I have diabetes) I ate them all. And, when Mama found me, I had chocolate all over my mouth.

"What happened?" she asked me.

All I could do was show her the bag where the chocolates were. And, the proof was all over my mouth. I was guilty without a fair trial. My mama spanked me well, but did I learn from that? Again, and again Mama spanked me when I did not listen or when I got into trouble; in my case, it was all the time.

The next time was for being too nice to the neighborhood kids. Every mid-afternoon, Mama put us down for a "*Siesta*" two hours at least, especially when it was around the summer days. While everyone took a nap, I sneaked out of the house and went to play with the neighborhood children. The *paletero* (ice cream man) was coming around the corner when we all got excited, but no one had any money. I spontaneously said, "*Mi mama esta rica, orrita vengo!*" (My mama is rich, I'll be right back!) And, yes, I purchased *paletas* (popsicles) for the kids with my mama's hard-earned savings. The amount of money I spent was not a lot; the paletas cost a minimum of five to ten cents. However, just the fact I pulled this sneaky business. There was no escaping my mama's favorite punishment, the belt. I could tell you countless troubles I got into, but I rather stop there. Because, by now, I am sure you agree with me that the name of this chapter fits.

Keep in mind that I was not the only child. Mama had four other children to take care of. Not to mentioned, Sergio was ill and needed Mama's attention 24/7. Sergio was the eldest of the five but needed all her attention. Sergio, at nine months young, became ill from meningitis, ever since then, his body was developing and growing, but his brain was as a baby. My oldest sister, Angela she listened to Mom; she was in school. Luis Fernando, two years older than me, also listened well to Mama. When he also went to school, he and his sister would walk together. Luis Fernando was thin and fragile, that if anybody picked on him, Angela would defend him; she did not care what anybody said about her; she would whip any guy's butt if needed. This brings me to my younger brother, Daniel. He and I stayed home with Mama.

Well, now you know Mama had her hands full. As I said, she warned me to stay away from the *bruja's* house and kids. Unfortunately, I did not listen again. Regardless of all that, I did nothing wrong to deserve what I experienced with the bruja's children., I had no clue what was going on. How did I know two kids, same age as my brother and sister, would want to harm me? I was too young to know right from wrong, and obviously, I was too hard-headed. During the years, our family lived next door to the bruja, her son and daughter, who were older than me by three or four years. My mama was trying to tell me for a reason not to play with these older children, but I did not listen. I do not even remember their names. But I do remember that I would sneak out of the house to go and play. My mama called me a "*Vaga*," which means a wanderer.

Well, I was about five years old, and, yes, my mind wandered. Anyhow, I would go and play with the *bruja's* children. The first time I recall was when they were playing hide and seek. Their parents had an old station wagon parked in the back of the house. Their backyard was very big. Unlike the tract homes here in California, every home in San Luis was built on huge lots. I recall that we were playing some game like I was their daughter and they were my parents, and I just remember the boy and the girl removing my pants and underwear and, with a toothpick, they poked and explored my genital and anal areas. They caused me pain, and most of all, I felt a weird sensation. This occurred maybe twice. I do not have clear memories of it. All I know is I felt bad and did not want to be around them anymore. I avoided them as much as possible and never said a word to anyone, not to my mom, sister or anybody.

I never shared these experiences with anyone. Now that I remember, it feels like maybe I am making things up in my mind. It is terrible to feel those memories; it is bad triggers. But I kept telling myself all these years that it did not happen. So, I did not think about it. But the more I tried and tried to forget; it kept coming back, causing me to feel dirty and guilty. I can't blame anybody for this; who knows what kind of childhood they were dealing with? Their mother was pretty bad, she would beat them, and they did not have friends because no one in that neighborhood got along with their mother. I am completely at peace with myself about this. Because I now know that it was not my fault like I used to think it was. I thought because I did not listen to Mama, it was a punishment, but there is no such thing. I know my mother's prayers and God's mercy has had a lot to do with my recovery and wellbeing. I had a great childhood, much better than those two kids did.

I just want to share this because no child anywhere should stay silent when any situation makes them feel uncomfortable. No matter what it is, all should speak up. Now that I'm qualified to talk about the effects that sexual abuse and other types of child abuse do on a child, I understand the consequences of an abused individual. As many times I blamed myself for what had happened to me. The symptoms that I grew up with were anxiety and depression, symptoms that, as a child, you cannot possibly understand. Then later feeling the sense of low self-esteem, leading to helplessness and just thinking, "I know, this is what I deserve because I am no good for nothing; a total flake or a loser." That feeling is absolutely awful.

It was unfortunate that this happened to me, but despite that, I have great childhood memories. I did say all the other neighbors were nice, right? Yes. They sure were. We played many games like *la rona* (tag), *canicas* (marbles), *beisbol* (baseball) and we went swimming in the canals. There were times Mama would let us stay outside with a bon fire on, telling chilling *cuentos*, like *La Llorona* and other scary short stories. Mama always took care of us since Papa was either working nights or was away in California.

I can honestly say that I was Daddy's little girl. Papa used to call me *la prieta (brownie)* or *la flaca* (skinny) since I used to be thin and darker skin as opposed to my sister Angela, who was very light skin. Nevertheless, when he was home, Papa took me with him everywhere he went. In those days, Papa worked at a nightclub in San Luis near the border called *El Riviera*. On Sundays, Papa would go in the morning to clean up, before opening again, when the night before was too hectic. Papa took Luis and Daniel with him to help him clean up. Afterward, the other workers and us would go play *beisbol*, and then we would go eat Tacos de Cauhuma (Sea turtle tacos) before sea turtles became extinct. It was an all-day thing and so much fun.

I also remember one of my birthdays because Mom bought me a coconut cake. It was the best cake I ever tasted. I remember going with Mama that day; we went across the border and spent most of the day grocery shopping. I enjoyed going with Mama because she would buy me and Daniel ice cream and let us ride the mechanical horse rides or cars. As a matter of fact, when I turned five, my mama took me to a photographer's studio and had my picture taken standing next to a cake. This is the only picture I had of mine when I was little. The cake was not even a real cake, it was made of paper, and my dress was made by Mama from scraps of cloth she had from making curtains and blankets. But I love this picture; when I see it, it reminds me of a happy little girl who was ambitious, a dreamer, and spontaneous. Regardless of despairs, poverty, and my dysfunctional family, I absolutely had a great life. But little did I know back then that studies now show that children who suffer from poor economic conditions and separations from a parent for a significant period of time. Those children are at risk for the following; lower levels of educational achievement, twice as likely to drop out of school, more likely to become teen parents, more likely to become truants, more frequently abuse drugs and alcohol, higher-risk of sexual behavior, and more likely to join a gang. I know this now, and I understand much of my life's choices. But during my childhood, there were some fun times.

When I was six years old, I almost had the opportunity to see my idol, Juan Gabriel. He was about twenty years old and had just started out signing his first hits like "*No Tengo Dinero*" and "*Uno, Dos, y Tres*." He visited a radio station in San Luis around 1973, and I was so excited. But there were so many people at the radio station; it was smaller than a box. I was never able to get in, not even, to the front door. But Angela did; she even got to sit on his lap and have her picture taken. I envied her so much for that and thought that was the coolest thing ever.

I enjoyed seeing Juan Gabriel sing; no matter what people said about him, I love and respect him as a talented composer from Mexico. I admired his professional career as a singer, composer, and entertainer. He did so much for the people of Mexico. His story is truly encouraging and amazing. After all, he lived through in his childhood and young adult life; he had so much to offer as he always had been a very humanly and caring person. It would have been an honor to have met him. May he rest in peace; Alberto Aguilera Valadez died in August 2016.

Well, my fun days soon came to an end because I had to start school. I turned six years, and I was enrolled in first grade. Every day was torture, not being with Mama and hanging around with her and Daniel, I knew exactly what I was missing, the ice creams when shopping at "El Otro Lado" (across the Border) San Luis, Arizona was just a few steps across the border, and everyone who had a permit could cross and drive all the way to Yuma to shop and visit as long as you didn't prolong your stay without a special permit. Since Mama did not drive, we just walked to the stores in San Luis Arizona, to buy the groceries, and Mama would let me and Daniel ride the mini horsey carousel.

All that was over for me, and well pretty much for the first two weeks when my first year of school started, I would act up when all the students lined up before entering the classroom. I always choked, cried, or fainted. Yes, I caused many teachers to hate me. I would have anxiety, but I did not know; nobody knew. The teachers were on me; they assumed I was faking it to get out of going to school. They figure out that I was like 'the little girl who cried wolf' in the long run, all that just got me in trouble. It was a matter of getting used to. But no teacher had any consideration or sympathy for me. What it did for me was for no one to ever, believe me, no credibility for all long time, with family, teachers, and classmates. I had a bad reputation. Did I mention the teachers were very mean? Mexican schoolteachers back in those times did not have a clue of how to treat a child, or scientifically know like what many professionals know today regarding an absent parent or what happens to a child when separation from a parent. Dr. Bowlby wrote books on the area of separation anxiety disorders and attachment. One is called A Secure Base: Parent-Child Attachment and Healthy Human Development, and another are Maternal Care and Mental Health; both of these explanations and talk about what a child goes through at such point of separation from a parent or maternal care as in my case when I separated from my mother to go to school and the separation of my father when he would leave to work in the U.S.A.

The symptoms of a Separation Anxiety Disorder are:

1. Recurrent excessive distress when separation from home or major attachment figures occurs or is anticipated.
2. Persistent and excessive worry about losing major attachment figures occur.
3. Persistent and excessive worry that an untoward event will lead to separation from a major attachment figure.
4. Persistent reluctance or refusal to go to school or elsewhere because of fear of separation.
5. Repeated complaints of physical symptoms (headaches, stomachaches, nausea, vomiting, etc.) when separation from major attachment figures or is anticipated. And much more other types of symptoms concerning this anxiety disorder. These are all, according to Dr. Bowlby. But nobody believed me; everyone thought I was a big fake. I do remember when my papa would leave back to the United States to work, I would write him a

letter, telling him how much I missed him, yet it was not even a few hours that he had departed. That is how sad it was for me not to be able to see my father for months and months up to a whole year or two.

One day I was taught a lesson. That morning, I was walking to school from my house, alone. The house and the school were about three blocks apart. Well, this crazy man followed me, and I noticed he was catching up to me. When I ran faster, he would too. When he finally got closer to me, he pulled down his pants and exposed his penis to me. I ran to the school and told one of the teachers, and she said, "Of course he did, Lidita, *Vete ha to salon de clase.*" She said, "sure he did," in a very sarcastic way, then she yelled at me, "Lidita, get to your class room!"

I pretty much stopped sharing things with people and kept to myself. I either had the choice of crying wolf or just "suck it up." So that is what I did. Having friends was out of the question. I knew that the reason why they did not take me seriously was my entire fault. I had dug my own grave. Everyone in school saw me and treated me as the girl who over-exaggerated on things, and no one wanted to hang around with a liar and *chillona!* (Cry baby). It was tough going to school in Mexico. You either lived with the agony and tough it out or have a big brother or big sister to protect you. I had both but no protection; although my brother Luis did, he was weak as I was, but he did have my sister's protection. My sister was tough; there was a reason why she was tough. I will discuss later why she was so tough; she was the oldest. That is one reason, and maybe that was one of the main reasons, but it was maybe the foundation of her endurance, presently.

Well, at last, I learned my lesson, and my hard-headed started learning how to read and write. I remember one day I begin to read to Mama; she was very happy to hear me read. I should have just accepted her admiration, but no! I had to feel important, that day she sent Luis and me to a nearby market, which was down the block and to the corner from our house. Mama asked my brother to buy milk and eggs; she gave him some money and told him to bring back the change. While inside the store, I told Luis that Mama told me to buy candy as an award because she was proud of me for reading. When we got home, she found out that the big lie I had invented to my brother, my spot-award, was no longer available. Mama had to use her magic belt on me again! When was I going to learn? Ah, not for a long time. I just got started.

After some time, I turned eight years old, and we moved to the house Mama and Papa were building for us. We would be moving very close to the rest of Mama's family: Mama Nita and my mom's eldest brother and wife. At that time, this area was called *La Aviacion*. The greatest thing besides moving close to our other cousins and Grandma was that this meant I would go to a new school! Yes! I had the opportunity to make friends. By then, I learned to like school and was no longer dependent on Mama. I tried hard to stay quiet. But I could not shut up, like the way I still am. However, the last thing I wanted was to be annoying to the other students. So, I waited for them to talk to me first. I was so excited to have friends again. I wanted to have friends; I wanted to be liked and to fit in; which child doesn't?

The home we moved into was new. Actually, it was not completely built. But Mama told Papa that before he left for California again, she wanted to move into the new home since she was now afraid of living in the old neighborhood, where many gangs had moved into some abandoned structures across the street from our house. Even though the house was not yet finished, we moved in. Some of the floors were not done, and a few windows were missing. But we managed to move into two of the rooms. The plan was that as soon as Papa crossed the border, he would be sending Mama the money to finish the home once he started working in California. Very soon after we moved into the house, Papa left for the United States.

Months after we settled into our new home, out of nowhere, San Luis got hit with a bad storm. It was a combination of rain and strong winds; it was called a Cyclone. I remember that day very clearly as if it were yesterday. My sister Angela, my brothers, Luis, Daniel, and I were hanging around, playing, in the family station wagon that Papa left abandoned. We were playing pretend as if we were riding on a trip when we felt the station wagon rocking, moving side to side. The rain was hitting hard, too. Initially, we were very scared to get out, but we got out safely and ran into the house. To our surprise, our mama was dealing with a bigger problem in the house. Mama had been screaming from the top of her lungs to help her. Sergio, our oldest brother, was sitting on a small couch, completely unaware of what was going on. Sergio, during the time of the storm he was about sixteen years old. I'm pretty sure he was scared because Mama was holding a piece of plywood that was used to cover the window; since we had moved in with the home not fully completed, well, let's just say, these were the consequences.

When we walked in, we heard her screaming our names, and when we saw what she was doing, we ran to help her, but the wind was much too strong; as soon as we let go of the plywood, the roof lifted, too. We felt like the "Three little pigs" when the big bad wolf huffed and puffed and blew the house down.

Mama sent Fernando (Luis) to get help at our tio's (uncle's) house. Fernando was about 80 lbs, and when he was running, he looked like he was flying.

After the winds calmed down, *our tio* sent one of his sons, Tony, to pick us up and take us to Mama Nita's house, where our stay turned out to be for three months, until the home was redone and completed correctly. It turned out that the joists that supported the roof were done improperly and, the strength of the winds coming in through the window blew the already weak section of the roof off. We also found out that San Luis Sonora was hit with the tail end of a cyclone. We were more than lucky to have just lost the roof. Some people lost their lives. Thank you, *Dios mio* (my God), for not blowing us away.

I was always the troublemaker of the family, and one of my troubles I got us in while we lived for a short period of time with our Mama Nita. It was when I was playing with *el Primo* (cousin) Siri. We were playing in the front yard, forming a house of dirt and piling mountains. We moved the dirt around with shovels when he said to me, "*Ahorita regreso.*" I thought Siri had gone inside his house, Mama

Nita's and my uncle's house, and her son's house were connected like a duplex. My mom and my cousin's mom were visiting Mama Nita in her house. I freely swung the shovel and accidentally struck his right eyebrow, he was still standing behind me, and I didn't know.

Well, Mama was always scared of *tio*, her brother, well actually everyone in the family was. I guess he always was up tight about something; he managed Mama Nita's land and his own and worked at an agricultural office. When Mama found out what happened, Siri heard Mama asking his mom, tio's wife, "What's going to happen to us? My brother is going to run us away from his house, and our house is not ready. Where are we going to go when he finds out what Lidia did to Siri?"

That evening, when my tio came home, he saw Siri's right-side eye bandage up (Siri had gotten ten stitches) and asked him, "What happened, Son?" (*Hijo, Que te Paso?*)

Siri answered him. "*Me pegue en la pared.*" (I bumped my head onto the wall.) He was only six years old, but he already had a caring heart. Luckily, despite my tio's grouchiness, my tio had a compassionate heart, too, or his wife's pleading for my mother and our family. As he possessed a good heart also, and he handled the situation well. He understood that we were just two kids playing, and accidents *do* happen. And, luckily for me, tio could think in realistic terms because I later injured another one of his sons.

So, after our house was livable, we moved back into it and settled in. It was great; brand new roof, mosaic floors, and nice new windows. Mama even purchased new furniture. We felt like the families on TV, where their homes are remodeled, and when they come back, they are in for a wonderful surprise.

Okay, so we were in school; everything went well, a whole school year had gone by, I made some friends and managed to stay out of trouble for a bit, when here I go, again. One day after school was out, when walking next to my cousin's Pita's cousin, the boy I met during the summer vacation at *El Barrote*, where my tia Lidia lived and owned a mini-mart called *La Pina*. The house was near a canal that was behind her home, along with three other homes. Tia Lidia would worry for the children constantly. Her concern was because while she tended the customers at the grocery store, the kids would run out of the house and play near the big canal that was behind their property. So, she asked me to come and keep my cousins, Pita, and her little brother, company. I was nine years old by then; I did not even know what I was really supposed to do other than have fun with them; I was a kid myself.

My mom was asked if I could stay with them since it was summertime and we were not in school. So, I ended up helping out my Tia Lidia because I would keep the kiddies entertained, watching cartoons, coloring, and playing hide and seek. One day I tried making flour tortillas. This was interesting because that was not what I was told to do. I heard my tia telling us, "When you kids get hungry, there is food already prepared on the stove; just make some flour tortillas," But what she actually said, "Just come inside the store and get a pack of flour tortillas," I still remember her telling me to make flour tortillas. But how, If I did not know how to make them. I just lead myself with memory when I use to see Mama make tortillas for my siblings and me. I had an idea what the ingredients were, but the more water I would pour into the bowl, the more flour I would need. It was just not coming out right; I had my two cousins, Pita and Tito, busy, one pouring warm water and the other adding flour, while my hands vigorously kneaded; busy with my two hands mixing the dough and then, literally, we were caught with the hands in the *Masa*! That's a saying in Spanish when someone is caught in the midst of committing a crime. Except that this masa was not ready to make tortillas, it looked more like we were making *Engrudo* (paste). It was runny and sticky.

When tia walked in, she screamed, "What in the world are you kids doing?" Her kitchen was a complete mess; we dirtied so many dishes, all for nothing. When we turned around, we saw her holding the package of tortillas, the ones we were supposed to get so we could eat. "I guess that is why I still do not know how to make tortillas" I traumatized myself. I can't even bake.

So that very summer, I met a boy, my cousins' cousin, he was about four years older than me, and he was nice to us; he would swing us on the swing set and make sure we did not fall off the slide. His full name is actually Josue. However, his family called him Joey. After that little masa fiasco, my stay with my cousins came to an end. I was sent back home; I was just another child for my aunt to care for. I really don't know what they were thinking, that an eight-year was supposed to care for two younger children?

After that, when we returned to school, I would see Joey around school and knew now who he was. And, on one particular day, Joey and I were walking parallel to each other. I do not recall if we were talking, and if we were, what we talked about. For some reason, cousin Eddie, who was about 15 feet away, was walking toward his house, yelled to me, "*Eje le eje le, la* Lidia *con su novio!*" He was making fun of me, like if I had something to do with this boy as if Joey was my boyfriend.

I was embarrassed And, I knew he was not my *novio*. Eddie's accusations really made me angry. I picked up a rock and threw it at him. Though we were some distance apart, the anger I felt made my strength powerful, and the rock landed on top of his head, causing the skin to break. Little did I know that in the future, Joey was going to be my boyfriend. If I had a crystal ball, I would have avoided pain for both Eddie and me.

Immediately, he ran, crying to his house. I, too, ran to my house crying, but I was crying because I knew that as soon as I would tell Mama what I'd done, she would not take it lightly.

Sure enough, she was watering the front yard when I got home. As soon as I saw her, I told her what happened. She immediately grabbed the end of the *manguera* (water hose) with enough length to use as a belt and landed it against my butt! She struck me three times, yelling at me, "What have you gotten me into, knowing well how your tio gets mad and reacts?"

I cried so much and went to sleep it off. When I woke up, it was like 8 pm, and Mama called me into the kitchen to eat dinner. After she and I talked, I knew that Mama was not mad at me anymore. I guess the injury to Eddie's head was not that serious because nothing else was mentioned after that.

This was the last time I would get into trouble, at least in Mexico. Because that year, before the school year ended, Mama announced to us that we would be moving to join Papa in California. Just when I was continued to make some friends and learning things, I enjoyed doing it. I have recited poems with my friend Roberto Canto, who, by the way, I had a crush on. I was in third grade, and my teacher's name was Matutina. She had a very pretty, light complexion. And, best of all, she liked me.

I also volunteered to sing in front of all the other students during the morning when we saluted the flag and when talent shows were held once a month. One of the songs I remember that was very popular was one of my favorites of Juan Gabriel's "*Tu estas siempre en mi mente*" (you are always on my mind).

My saddest time before we moved to America was that on the last week of classes, I signed up for a talent show, and I had just the song. It was, of course, by one of my favorite singers, Juan Gabriel, "*Tu estas siempre en mi Mente*." As soon as class was out, I ran home to change into a dress, a hand down from my cousin, Eddie's, and Siri's older sister.

The dress was long, and it fit me kind of loose, but it was beautiful. By the time I got to my house and finished getting ready and ran back to school, two hours had passed. I got to the school and to my surprise, when I got to the school, the talent show was over! It had started right after school was out. I do not know why I never heard the announcement.

The janitor saw me looking through the locked gates, so I asked him to let me in.

When he said, "No, young girl, it's over," I was crushed.

All of my dreams came down on me that day. I felt like an idiot; I was embarrassed even though no one saw me, except for the janitor was the only one to see me in that long dress. It was humiliating enough, just to imagine what my teacher and classmates thought of me. So, that was the end of my artistic days in San Luis. But I was not the only one who sang. One day Manuel, my youngest brother, surprised us all when he sang, "*El Rey*." Daniel was six years old and in first grade. He could barely talk and reach the microphone. However, he was able to belch out the high notes of the song of one of Mexico's greatest composers, Jose Alfredo Jimenez. One of my youngest cousins would pick on Daniel and say he was "*Chiquiado*" (spoil rotten). Daniel was the youngest and the child in our family who spent the least amount of time with Dad, so he was very close to Mama like he still is today. So, that was the end of both my brother's and my artistic days in San Luis.

All About Moving to America

The school year ended, and Mama already warned us that we were moving to California. Mama had also talked with our Mama Anita and her brothers and sisters. The sisters wished her the best, but the brothers were kind of negative toward her decision. She told them that we all needed to be together, with Papa. She said, "The children are growing, and I need his help to raise them. I can't do it alone."

The day that we were packing our clothes, she said to us, "Do not take too many clothes, just a couple of pairs of every item, we are not going to stay forever." Those words were very inspiring because we did not want to leave our house; we all wanted to live near our family, our friends, our life was in Mexico.

Mama had a different plan for us. A plan that she only knew, not even Papa, knew what was going through Mama's mind.

My sister Angela was turning 15th the following year, which meant that there were no plans to celebrate the traditional Quinceanera. I am sure that was very painful for her. And just imagine what was going through every child's mind while our mom was in action. And just like my sister was suffering, so was my brother Luis Fernando, he was not with us anymore, Mama had already packed his clothes and sent him across the border to stay with some friends in San Luis, Arizona. I was sad, scared and at the same time excited to see Papa and see all the places he talked about when he would come to visit (short stays in Mexico) in the past years. Daniel really did not say much he was six and was ready to go. Sergio was just rocking himself on his recliner chair, happy, content, and smiling.

The next morning a family member related to our Papa picked us up. It was Papa's niece and her husband, Pancho. They were very nice; they both had great respect toward Papa and admired Mama for being a wonderful wife and a mother.

The couple were younger and had two children Veronica and little Panchito; they were adorable children, well dressed, and very respectful. When they picked us up, we loaded our suitcases in their elegant, elongated light blue car.

The next thing we know is that we are in line to cross the border into *el otro lado* (across the border). Then came to our border patrol agent asked where we were traveling. Pancho said, "Me, my wife, and our children are giving this family a ride to the bus station in Yuma, Az. Because they are going on a vacation to Fresno, Ca." Then the agent asked for our names and asked for Mama's passport and permit to travel.

Mama has always been a very smart woman, and I think now that she knew more than me when I was her age. She knew it was the 4th of July and that the immigration department was working with very little crew. We, on the other hand, did not know what this day meant for

Americans. We just knew it was the only day they were allowed to burn fireworks. So, to us, this meant Day of the Fireworks.

Then, the agent, after Mama spoke to him, he begins to point at every single child; Mama called our names when she said my sister's name, Angela, little Panchito, said, "Her name is Angela, but we call her Kiko because she is crying. Kiko is another character who came out in the popular Mexican comedy show; I have previously mentioned '*El Chavo del Ocho*'. Kiko portrayed the character of a ten-year-old boy, and when things did not go his way, he would cry and throw a tantrum. This program is now over fifty years old, and most Latin channels around the world still air the shows. The border agent might have known who he was too because he laughed and told us to have a nice trip, giving us the signal with his right hand to pull forward and go."

We were actually not taken to Yuma; we only made a stop in San Luis, AZ to pick up brother Luis from our friend's house, they wished us lots of luck, and we went on our way. I guess they just had to say that we were getting dropped off in Yuma to avoid suspicion and confusion. We were taken to Brawley, California, where Pancho, his wife, and the kids dropped us off with another family member; at that point, we said goodbye to them too. We then waited for the night to arrive to continue our trip. We did not know why; as I said, Mama seemed to know exactly what she was doing. That evening we were picked up by another one of my dad's nieces and her husband. I do not remember their names, as we were not introduced.

The next thing we knew, we were traveling in a small red Datsun truck with a camper, Mama, Sergio, Angela,

Luis Fernando, Daniel, and me. We took blankets, few bags of clothes, and faith in our mama, that wherever we were going, it was for the best. Although my sister Angela knew this too, she was still very sad and felt crying was her only option. All I heard was Mama telling her to calm down, or she would get us into trouble. This was pretty confusing to me. All I knew we were coming to *Los Estados Unidos* to see our father. And some sprinkled fairy dust of hope "To better our lives."

And I soon learned what our mama was dealing with. We were all crossing with a pass port/visa to come to California, except for our brother, Sergio. He was not allowed to cross because he was sick, and immigration would not allow him into this country. Pretty much, he was crossing illegally, and if the border patrol agents at the checkpoint discovered him, it would be over for us.

As I said, Mama has always been a very clever woman, and she picked The Fourth of July purposely because, during that holiday, the *Migra* worked on a skeleton crew, sort-of speak. At the checkpoint, they let us go without an intense inspection. And that was how it happened. We were all asleep and covered with blankets when we crossed. At the 2nd inspection, the *emigrante*, looked at the permit/visa and did not bother to match the names with all the heads. Of course, Mama had been praying the prayer of *La Somrbra Del Señor San Pedro (a prayer To St. Peter) La magnifica* (The Magnificent), to our belief, is a very powerful prayer, all along the way.

The next stop was Los Angeles, the end of our ride in the back of the Datsun. Our next transportation was a Greyhound bus to Fresno. Meanwhile, we waited at the

Greyhound station. That was something else; it seems like it was like a whole new world for all of us. It was a lot different than *when just crossing to the otro lado, in San Luis, Arizona. To me*, people were different. There was a mixture of races. I had never seen that in my life.

At the bus station, there were a lot of people that scared me; they were sleeping like if they were living there, because they had bags with them and they appeared too confused, some were asking for money and food. Los Angeles was a big city from what we can see. But we only stayed a couple of hours. Mama looked tired and concerned when our brother Sergio would scream and cried out loud. It seemed that he was tired too and was already missing his recliner chair back home.

Our bus ride gave Mama another reason to worry and pray. Now, there were six of us and just five on the permit and it was daytime. If the *Migra* (Border Patrol agent) had checked, we would have been in trouble. Mom was like a mother goose. She kept counting heads and would push Luis Fernando under the seat every time the bus stopped because she did not know where the immigration checkpoint would be, and she wanted to be prepared.

I tell you, the prayer of the *Sombra del Señor San Pedro* helped. Because the *migra* did check the bus, and when Mama showed them the permit, they glanced where Mama pointed at us and did not match heads with names. We were clear to go.

When we arrived in Fresno, Papa and his *compadre* picked us up, and we went to a town called (where our new home would be) Kerman. We met our dad's compadre's family and his wife, who welcomed us and fed us our first meal. She was very nice and spoke very little Spanish, her way of speaking was as different as her cooking, she fed us her style of chicken mole and Spanish rice. Mom's mole was a lot different, but don't get me wrong, they were both tasty, just very different.

At last, the *familia* settled into a two-room home. Yes, a large bedroom and a kitchen. The large bedroom was a living room and also turned out to be the bedroom for the five children, Mama and Papa. Dad, who had lived in Kerman for the past four years, is where he brought us; according to him, there were no homes for rent. Anyways, "Here we all are, together again," I thought in my mind. And trying to make sense of things, I started to compare the current weather, it was summertime, and it was not as hot as we were used to. I don't recall how hot it was in the San Joaquin Valley; all I know it was not hotter than San Luis; that day when we left must have been like 115 degrees. In Kerman, it did not feel that hot. It must not have been because I was cold, which explains why I was wearing a sweater. Or maybe, that's how I was feeling, strange in a different country.

The move was a big thing; it meant leaving our friends and relatives. Even though we did not gather at Mama Nita's house, as much as we would have wanted to, we were still going to miss her. Mama Anita was not the most caring type of grandma that you can imagine; she had her favorite grandkids, but nevertheless, we loved her, and we were going to miss her.

Surpresa!

I remember my tenth birthday. I don't know if you had a memory or memories of your birthday celebrations when you were young? Maybe? Maybe not. Well, I do, my tenth birthday, I do.

We were still in this two-bedroom home, and I was given the chores of washing everybody's clothes. My mother started work the day after we arrived. And, of course, Dad was working too. Angela took care of Sergio. Luis and Daniel would, pretty much, play with *canicas* and hang around. It was a month after our arrival in the U.S.A. All I did the whole time was washed the entire family's clothes.

Well, my birthday came on a weekday. I remember that I spent the day with my mama and papa's *compadre's* wife, Tina. She was very nice. But she was a *pocha* and spoke very little Spanish, much like a *gringa* (Spanish Speaking white woman) would speak it. This reminded me of, "When We were kids, playing with our cousins, in San Luis, we would actually speak like if we were Pochos, speaking broken Spanish. That's how she sounded."

So, on this particular birthday, we drove into Kerman and went to the store. I was helping her with her two boys and little girl. When we got back to her house, she told me to go home and to let my family know to come back later.

I was completely hurt and did not understand why she would tell me to leave her house. It was as if *la tierra* (the land) had swallowed me alive.

Our home sat directly across the street from hers. To get to our house, I first had to pass the *empacdora de pasas* (raisin packing house). The name at that time was Melikian Raisin Packing. Well, at that particular time, Tio Miguel was also staying with us. Tio Michael is Papa's youngest brother; his family lived in San Luis too. And like dad, he was currently working staying with Papa to keep him company; he was actually planning to stay only through the working season and return to San Luis to his family. He was also working at the packing house during the night shift, so Tio Michael saw me crying and asked, "Porque lloras, hija?" (Honey, why are you crying?)

I told him, "Dad's compadre's wife asked me to leave her house and come back later." He asked, "La Pocha?"

"Si" (yes), I answer him. He said, "No llores" (do not cry). Maybe she has "*Una sorpresa*" (a surprise). Suddenly my cry turns into curiosity.

*O*h my God. What in the world was a '*Sorpresa?*'

"*¿Una sorpresa?*" I asked.

He nodded. "*Si, hija, un pastel con una piñata y regalos!*" ("Yes, honey, a cake, pinata and gifts.") "*una pachanga!*" (a Party)

I could not wait. The last time I had a cake on my birthday was when I was six. Mama took me to get my picture taken next to a fake cake. I wore the brand-new dress that my mama made for me, and my shoes were hungry.

(That's what we use to say when our shoes had holes on the tips.)

Tio Michael's kind words made me feel better. I did not know exactly what to expect. But, one thing for sure, I was no longer sad on my birthday.

A few hours later, the *familia* went to the *compadre's* house. And, to my surprise, literally, it was a 'sorpresa'. There was a cake with writing, "Happy Birthday, Lidia." There was food, *regalos* (gifts), and other family members of Tina whom I had never met before that day. But there was no *piñata*. Oh my God! This was the greatest day ever. This was the first time I was given training bras. She was just such a nice person, a very thoughtful and caring person. My name on my cake, my very own cake. It was so colorful, with purple, pink, and yellow flowers. My name was spelled wrong, but I loved it anyway.

This was when I began to spell my name L-y-d-i-a instead of L-i-d-i-a. To me, the new way was way cooler. I was not the only one who changed their name, by the way. My brother, Luis Fernando, was now L-O-U-I-S. Interesting. We were quickly becoming Americanized.

Life Starts in America

The summer was short; it was time to return to school. Tina helped Mama enroll all of us in school, except for Angela and, of course, Sergio. Since Angela was the oldest, Papa and Mama had her stay to take care of Sergio. By then, we moved out of the *secadora de pasas* (raisin Dehydrator). Mama convinced Papa to look for a bigger house. And, guess what? There was one for rent. I still remember the street, North Madera Ave, known as the main highway (145) in Kerman. Papa has always been a conformist, always doing the bare minimum. But he was doing the best he could when he was on his own. He was trying to deal with having the whole family at all at once. There were changes that were for sure, and Mama was about to change his world and ours too.

My parents had no knowledge of the laws of this new country. They were not aware that it was illegal to keep a minor from going to school. However, they soon learned.

Angela was sent to high school. Sergio was enrolled in a special education school. Aside from Mama wanting a better life for us, we had come to the Unites States because she wanted us all to be together as a family and the hope for our brother, Sergio. She thought maybe he would get better, or at least have improved medical healthcare. Unfortunately, his condition would never get better. He would never be a normal person. His medical condition was chronic, and those medical problems kept him much like a baby. But Mama did get one wish come true for Sergio. He got better healthcare. But later, he was put into a hospital. Never again did Mama have to care for him or worry about who would when she had to work. I know mom thought of Sergio every day, and she hurt in silence. She is just a strong individual and knew she had four other children to get ahead. Although she worried about him every day, she kept her vision on her dream. I just did not know mom had dreams; a mother naturally has dreams and always worries about her children.

I admire Mama because she worked so hard and always thought she would someday have Sergio back with us, healthy and well. But that day never came. She finally accepted that he would have to stay in a convalescent home for the rest of his life. It was all about survival mode. She worked hard every day for us and settled by visiting Sergio once a month. Sergio lived to the age of forty years old. His illness was chronic, and one day he caught pneumonia. And, his ill and tired body just could not fight it any longer. Mom asked the physician that was caring for him right before he took his last breath that she approved for his organs to be donated for a person to be saved. The doctor was very grateful for my mama's decision.

Those are the sacrifices a family had to go through when wanting a better life. When she decided to bring us to the United States, she was not aware that through reaching goals and achievements, there be griefs and tears of sadness.

Nevertheless, soon we were all in school learning English, adjusting to a new school system, and trying to make sense of a new way of life.

Words Hurt More

I'm sure you have heard that a child's brain is like a sponge. Well, it is true. Soon, we were all speaking a new language besides our native language. But even though we could communicate with less difficulty, some of the other students made nasty remarks.

"Learn how to speak right, *mojada* (wetback)."

"You beaner."

These were all hurtful words. But, as children, you learn to endure and ignore sometimes. I was not the only one getting picked on. A group of others who started school with us did not speak a word of English. Some of them preferred not to speak in English at all in order to avoid being picked on for their lack of skill with the new language. The others were like me and did not care. At least we pretended not to care. Although I took the edge off my nerves by smiling, I cared. Because there were times, I preferred not to use words with "sh" or "ch" sounds. For example, instead of "Share," I would say "chair." It was embarrassing, and some even laughed at me. At those times, I went into the bathroom and cried in silence. That was not the only thing about me they made fun of. I was made fun of by my appearances.

(Nowadays, it's called bullying.)

I was developed fast. My breasts were bigger than normal girls my age, for an eleven-year-old. The boys called me "Bologna Boobs." Rather, I should say one boy. He had very dark skin and was Mexican, like me, except he spoke English. He was shorter than me, and his hair was dark black and greasy looking. I don't know if the other kids bullied him too. And that is how he would take it out on me. I do know that his voice was squeaky, like a mouse. I never liked to make fun of anybody, but when he would call me names, I would just smile and not appear to be bothered. I guess I really did not understand what he was saying. All I know, later he seemed to change his ways toward me, like not calling me names and such. I felt he respected me as a young girl. Actually, by the time I was in sixth grade, I felt it was getting a little better. Most of my classmates seemed to start to like me.

Well, everyone was nice except for my brother Luis. At home, he called me Dolly Parton. I knew that was how brothers were. But it made me furious. Little did I know that today, many Hollywood female figures with thick accents, and big boobs, like Sofia Vergara, have highly paid salaries. I read in a magazine where Sofia said during an interview that she always felt self-concession about her looks when she was a young girl, she said, because she was very thin and had big boobs. She told her mom that whenever she came of age, she would get them cut off. Well, we all know she did not. She makes lots of money with her looks and big chest. I, on the other hand, reduced my bust size and later in the years gained so much weight, just made me feel very miserable. Wow! So why did I not know this until now?

All I know is that, during those times, when young, it was awful. As awful as making friends again was, having to figure how to fit in was challenging; I felt like if I was back in school living in Mexico. At least in Mexico, everyone spoke the same language, and if someone was talking about me or making fun of me, I would understand why. I was never the fighting type. I did not like to make fun of anyone, but there was a young girl who was easy to pick on. She was sweet and belonged to a religious family, she always wore dresses to school, and I always felt jealous that she had nice dresses. Now that I think about it, they were like the dresses the little girls wore on the Little House of the Prairie shows. I would tell her so many mean things, like, "you don't look nice in that dress because you are not pretty," or "my cousins in Mexico wear nice dresses like that and they look pretty in them."

That was mean, right? Yeah, well, little did I know that this religious little girl had more than just God by her side, she was friends with this tough girl, and she must have been about two years older than us. I still remember when she approached me. We were on the bus. This girl had a mean type of look while she sat on the seat directly across from me. She waited for the bus driver to stop and get off to cross the children. Then, suddenly, I have her next to me, this girl breathing on my ear. She had a strong arm-pit smell, and she smelled like she had school lunch; she scared me just with that. But she looked at me; her nostrils were wider than ever; while pointing at a pocketknife in her pencil tin box, she says to me, "You know my little friend Lily?"

I cowardly answered her, "Yes."

"Well, you leave her alone. Next time I will use this on you!" She continued pointing at her pocketknife.

I never said anything to anyone in my school years. I understand why there is bullying. If one experiences it, then one can feel it is perfectly okay to take it out on someone else. Before you know it, it can really harm a child, young adult, and even older adults. I learned my lesson. I truly support every person that has been through what I have been through and who has been through worse than what I was put through.

I made friends with some girls that were from Mexico too. But they were from a different part of Mexico, places that I had only heard of when studying geography in San Luis while going to school. The other difference was that they spoke English longer than me, so they would help me with the pronunciation of words. The two girls were sisters; the youngest was in my grade. Her name in English was Hope. She was very smart and had long black hair, big bright black eyes as well as long eyelashes. I do not know where she is now, but I'm pretty sure she is doing great.

But my best friend was Hilda Mora. We were pretty close. In fact, she was like the first friend I ever had. Hilda moved with her parents, brothers, and sisters to Olympia Washington, she would write to me and send me pictures of her, but soon we lost contact. I do not know where she is now. I always think of her and miss her. I would love to someday find her to tell her all my life. I wonder if she thinks of me as much as I think of her. I have a picture she sent me that says, "To Lydia, my best friend, I will always remember you."

Oh, Dios Mio! What Is This?

The summer before starting school, the start of fourth grade, my menstrual period came. I had no idea what it was, and yet I was too embarrassed to tell my mama because I honestly thought I had done something bad. This is how naïve a young girl can be when their parents do not talk to them and prepare them for the body changes. Really! Every time I went into the restroom, I saw a purple box with a big print "Kotex," and I just had a haunch that those were to be used for this particular problem, along with bunches of toilet paper and three pairs of underwear, because I was afraid of staining my underwear. Oh, *Dios*! (Oh God!) This was a nerve-wracking day. Finally, I figured out how to use the pads, the cushioning part up, and the blue side down. Yes, for a while, I placed the adhesive side up, cushioning part down; the glue area was pretty uncomfortable.

Then, well, I finally got the courage to ask my sister and mama about this problem and realized that I was not pregnant, just because I had kissed a boy, yeah. I had kissed a boy in the mouth, and for some crazy reason, I thought I would get pregnant. Oh, *Dios!* (Oh God).

Part II

My Dreams; De Nina a Mujer (From Child to Woman)

We were all growing fast, and our parents both worked hard to provide for us. I remember we also helped our parents work during the summers. Luis, Daniel, and I worked picking grapes, turning and rolling trays. Every new school year, we had new clothes because we worked hard; I would buy every color of shoes you can think of, and my brother Luis dressed very GQ; he would buy the slickest pants and shirts. Daniel, on the other hand, liked to save his money and allowed Mama to dress him; he was always money-driven.

Mama tells us a story about when we lived in Mexico; she kept money put away in a cabinet drawer, she put money aside for emergencies and to pay for utilities, like to refill the gas tank. Daniel saw her pull out money from the drawer at one time. So well, one day, Mama needed the money to pay for the gas and pulled out the drawer, and the money was gone. "This time, it was not me." Maybe mom knew too because right away, she asked Daniel, and he said, "*Yo guarde Mama*" ("I put it away, Mom"), and he pulled out the money from an old sock from his box of *canicas* (marbles). My young brother always like to save his money, so whenever we "The big spenders," spent our hard-earned money, Daniel loaned us money and charged us interest or asked us to do something for him, like cook meals, clean his shoes, he would think of something, he later would remember. It was always fun hanging around with my brothers. We played cards, we named our stuffed animals, or got in trouble around the house while my parents were away at work. Our sister Angela would be the responsible person whenever we put a hole in the wall when horsing around the house or breaking a window; it never failed; she got in trouble. Sorry, Sister.

Mama always worked. She did not rest one day. She worked seven days out of the week and slept three hours a day. There were days during the summer when she worked four jobs at three packing houses and would run and help us pick grapes. That was insane. Mama taught us how to work hard and to achieve our dreams. Mama is the reason we are in America today. If she had listened to Papa and all the other negative people who told her she was crazy for wanting to move to another country, we would have stayed in Mexico, and who knows what would have happened to us. No one will know, but what we do know is that because of her courage, we are who we are today.

I compare my mama with "Alice from Wonderland" first because her name is Alicia which in English is Alice. Second, she is as beautiful as Alice, and lastly, she is a dreamer and brave as the Alice in the story. Mama is a very smart woman. She did not have the opportunities that I have had, and my daughters, nieces, and nephew now have. I'm pretty sure if Mama had studied in our era, she would have gone far. Thank you, Mama! You sacrificed your life when you gave me life and when you left your native country to give me a better life.

Although when growing up both Mama and Papa worked hard to make sure we had a roof over our heads, clothes to wear, and food on our table. As a young teen, I felt that it was not enough. I wanted to learn to dance, to model, to play an instrument, and to act. I had little or no support from my parents. I do recall the only thing my papa bought me was a clarinet, at a pawn shop, in the Fulton Mall area, next to the old Coney Island Restaurant. He had no Idea if it was working properly, and neither did I. But he bought it for me. And after a few music classes at school, that clarinet was set aside, never to be played again; I do not think I was good at playing it, but I tried, there was an incident that did occur while I was in band class, which I will later explain. Nevertheless, my envision did not stop there. I also remember looking up in the phone book places for dance and ballet lessons because I would hear other young girls in my classroom talk about dance classes and piano lessons, and others would say they were enrolled in Barbizon Modeling School. Back in that time, this was pretty popular. So, I wanted that too.

But, when I'd asked my parents, they simply said, "*No tas loca o que?*" and "This is how I would feel." How could I even think that I would be allowed? I would never get support from my hard-working parents, which were doing everything to help us survive in this new country that did not belong to us? Was I ungrateful? Why would I take their hard-earned money and ask them to pay for a dance lesson, ballet? Piano lessons? Model? I am pretty sure my parents really thought I was *loquita* (crazy).

At that time, I did not understand it. That whole sacrifice thing or listen to my inner voice. And if you do have an inside voice, you learn to ignore it. Yes, Soon, I ignored my dreams and just lived one day at a time. No more plans, no more dreams, just live. I did not know what my full potentials were or even recognize if I had any. I was just living and growing.

Then you begin to accept things as they come at you. Like being noticed by boys and, of course, if you all can recall how it feels when someone tells you that he or she likes you and sends you notes that say, "Do you want to go around?" Well, they may not use those exact words nowadays, but you know what I mean someone is paying attention, and it feels great! Yeah, well, I should have been persistent with my parents about the dance lessons and doing what I liked doing. But, when you're young, it is easy to be discouraged and get distracted if you constantly do not have someone keeping you interested. That is the reason I would say to myself, If I have children, I will never say no when it comes to doing sports, or any hobbies they want to do, dance, sing, ballet, model whatever as long as they are happy and they love what they are doing, that is completely their choice, and my only position is to support them. Actually, my papa did hear me when I asked to be in the school band, which is why he bought me the clarinet.

I used to think I would get married, have children and live in a nice home, and live happily ever and ever after. I have always been a dreamer. Mama allowed me to have a boyfriend at age 14; the wrong move, Mama! I was learning to play clarinet, dance, Folklorico, and performing in talent shows. I also enjoyed running track, hurtles, playing volleyball, and basketball. Having a boyfriend just lost me, plus my music teacher, Mr. Strickland, was a pervert, and I did not even know it. (Here is the story of why I quit the band). By that age, I was more than developed; I was a full-blown "*Señorita Bonita*," brunette, long legs, slim, and very heavy on the chest. He would call me in to meet him in the music room during my lunch hour, supposedly, to teach me how to play new music notes that I was not learning. The whole time I was in there with him, I could not even learn; he would get so close to me, his breath smelled like an ash tray, and he would kiss my cheek after we were done practicing. I felt uncomfortable. I was so confused. I did not know what to do, so, I did what felt right to do, I quit. I became a rebel and just hung around with some of the trouble makers at school and met with my boyfriend; he was a junior in high school when I was in eighth grade. The high school bus would come to our school site, Sun Empire, and pick us up along with the high school students. That is how I met him, plus he was already my brother Luis's friend. He would visit Luis at home, and that's how our romance started. When Mama found out about Brent and me, she said it was okay to see him. I was just not allowed to go anywhere alone with him unless Angela went with us to chaperone or when we all of us, as a family, would go out. That was good, that is the way it should be or even better, do not have a boyfriend at all at that age, which is much better. Papa did not agree; he'd much rather preferred I not to have a boyfriend. I guess I was always his little girl to him.

I remember one time Brent and I were in the dining room watching television. The kitchen had a pocket door that leads to the living room. That door was closed, and when Papa came into the kitchen, he saw us kissing. We were apprehended by surprise. So as soon as we saw him, we pushed away. Papa passed right by me; Brent was not looking at Papa because he was embarrassed. But Papa called my attention as he passed through to exit into the washroom area; he slightly kicked me and signaled me with his right hand's fingers that he had his eye on me. I was scared; I knew I had done it; as soon as he left, he screamed at me, not to do it again. Right? But of course, that continued. Now I think differently.

There will be plenty of time for that. The best thing to do is focus on what you like to do and study, study, and study. Papa was right; it is interesting because now I sit down and talk with Papa and share with him that I tell my Girls what he used to tell me and did not listen.

When I was in high school, this so-called boyfriend confessed to me that my brother Luis, some friends, and he went to the movies. Well, Brent confessed to me that he cheated on me with a girl from school; she was sort of my friend. Ronnie, I was even in her quinceanera! I did not even get to have one, well, my sister either, but this friend did. I only have a picture of me when I turned 15; I painted my face like a clown. I still do not know, maybe because I liked clowns. Oh well, regarding my cheating boyfriend and my so-called friend, I really do not know what exactly happened between them on that night, but he did say that her mouth and lips were much smaller than mine and her breasts were much bigger than mine. What a jerk!

I was fifteen by this time, and even though we were not having sex, we were making out, and other sexual things happened, of which I am ashamed to admit. I know I should have had more respect for myself. As far as my boyfriend, I did not break up with him after his confession. Yes, very stupid.

Well, that problem kind of took care of itself because the whole family had to move away pretty fast. In December of that same year, the immigration came and picked us up, except for Papa, because he was at work. At that time, we were living in Kerman on West Belmont Ave. The house belonged to this nice farmer, he was Russian, and he was a kind man, who appeared to like us very much. His wife seemed a bit stuck up, but you could tell she did whatever he ordered.

On the morning when two border patrol agents came, Mama was out in the front yard grabbing some wood logs to start up the fireplace when two INS agents surprised her. We were all getting ready to go to school. Since it was a foggy day schedule, we were waiting for the time to catch the bus. They came into the house with Mama and said in Spanish, "*Agarwren toddo lo que puedone, porque se van a un paseo to Mexico*" (grab your clothes and all things you can, because you are leaving to Mexico). The immigration agents even suggested that if we spoke English, we could be back in the U.S.A. fast. "This is what they told us on when riding in their white patrol car, on the way to the holding Border Patrol station."

"And that is exactly how it happened."

Well, before we were taken back to San Luis, Sonora, we were held in a small cell for a few hours. I still see it every day when I drive past by the old Golden State Blvd, just south from Shaw, very close to where The Marquez

Brothers Mexicanos building is. That little building is no longer an INS holding cell, but I still can see my family and I sitting in there eating hamburgers from Carl's Jr. because the agents asked us what we wanted, and they were kind enough to get us some lunch. We paid for them, with our own money, of course. My brothers, sister and I were not worried, we were ready to have some great *vacaciones*, with the *familia* that we had not seen since we left in 1977. I guess it is true what they say about first impressions. The immigration agents treated us very nicely; they did not mistreat us or make us feel unwanted. They were simply doing their job, there was a report against us, and it had to be followed according to their rules and policy, and it was.

The next day we arrived in Mexicali, which is a nearby town, an hour or two from San Luis. Nothing looked familiar because my siblings and I had never been to Mexicali, so this town was new to us. From there, we took a bus that took us to our hometown, San Luis; our whole family was surprised by our arrival. Once we arrived it, all began to look familiar. Besides, many of our cousins that were our same age were now older like us, and the ones that were just babies were older and cute. We also met new cousins that were born during our absence. It was all so wonderful to see our family eat the food we were so used to, as carnitas, tacos, churitos, flautas, coctel de camarones, cahuama and you name it, we ate to our heart's content. This was also when Daniel discovered his love for popping *cuhetes* (fireworks).

During this visit, Luis and Angela became *padrinos* (Godparents) of our youngest cousin, Lali; she was so precious. She was just under one year old, and her parents, our aunt and uncle, Juanita, and Margarito, asked them to baptize her. They just felt it was meant to be. And it worked out just wonderful. Luis loved Lali and felt proud to be a part of her world. He carried her Baptismal picture in his wallet all the time.

I did say we had a great time, right? It was like old times. Christmas in Mexico and New years were so fun. We made *lumbradas* (bomb fires) every night. Our aunts, mom, and Mama Anita made Tamales and all the other traditional food like Menudo and Pozole during the Navidad Season. We sang and danced with all our *tios* (uncles) and cousins to all the traditional Mexican party songs, like *La Loa, El Nino Perdido, La Yaquecita*, and much more. I didn't think we could ever have those times ever again. But those specific vacations made it possible; those days made our lives feel easier when we were back in the United States. At least for me, it did for a long time. I felt that I was loved, and no matter how far away I was from them, they always thought of me and I of them.

A few days after our arrival in Mexico, Papa came to see us make sure we were okay, but I could not understand why he would go and leave us. He went to his hometown in Guadalajara, Jalisco, Mexico. Mama explained to us that he took advantage of visiting his family, too, since it had been many years since he last saw his brothers and sisters. Our papa had arrived with his Compadre Benito, his wife Tina (la Pocha), and their children. Yes, my boyfriend at that time too, Brent also came with them. It was quite a scandal because he did not speak a word of Spanish, and my family was all giving him a hard time. He was so white, blonde hair and green eyes, when he was embarrassed, he would turn red like a tomato. He soon began to make friends with my male cousins. Luis and Daniel were his translators and helped him to make new friends.

We actually did not feel anything against the immigration department; they had to do what they were ordered to do. But, in our hearts, we thanked them for their suggestion. Yes, the whole family made it back, again, but this time not in Kerman. Our parents decided for all of us to move to Fresno because we did not want to be deported again.

I did not want to go to any other school besides the one I knew in Kerman; my parents would take me to school in the morning before they went to work and then pick me up after work. My brother, Luis, had no problem going to a new school in Fresno. He preferred not to face anyone that knew of our situation. The least, the better, because he felt embarrassed about the way we were taken to Mexico. Kerman was a small town, and everyone knew that we were *mojados*, or wetbacks, how we were called because of our illegal status. I did not care. But, soon, my parents forced me to finally transfer out from Kerman to Fresno High.

In life, one learns that things always happen for a reason.

But on this certain morning, I did not feel that way. Normally, Luis and I went to school on the bus together. But, on September 28, 1983, we did not. Papa, Mama, and Angela would leave to work as early as 5am. So my two brothers and I spent time together before we headed out to school every morning. My youngest brother had already left for school. But, not Luis and I. As we were getting ready for school, Luis asked me to make his favorite BLT sandwich.

After we ate, he asked me if I wanted a ride to school, and I declined, telling him I was going on the school bus (That particular day, school classes started later). I could have gone with him, as I knew I had time, but I decided to go to school earlier.

Luis's classes started later, as well as mine. But he was going to go to his ROP class at Hughes and Nelson by the Coroner's office. Luis would borrow Angela's car and would later end up at Fresno High. By then, I would get a ride home. But that is not how this particular day took the course.

I normally saw Louis around the school campus. But, this day, I did not see him in the usual spots he frequented with his buddies between the class periods or during lunch. After school, I took the Fresno City Bus from McKinley and Palm, across the street from Seven–Elven (It is unbelievable that the store has been there forever). I have good memories of that store. My friend Tessie and I would frequently walk there during breaks and bought one Caramelo and one big Gulp Soda. Sweet! Okay, so as soon as I got home, I noticed Angela's car parked on the lawn, which gave me an indication that Luis was home. I walked up the front steps; I must have rung the doorbell for five to ten minutes at the same time, walking back and forth to the backyard. After not getting a response from Luis, I thought maybe he was not home (remember, this is the '80s, no cell phones!) So then, I just wanted to get in. I decided to crawl in through the kitchen window. The house's foundation a bit high, so I had to use a woken box to be able to lift myself enough to reach up to the window sill and then landing onto the kitchen's sink.

Once I stepped into the kitchen, I heard music coming from the stereo in the dining area. As I passed the hallway by our parents' room, I saw Luis; there he was lying on Mama and Papa's bed. I yelled out, "Hey, you lazy bum, why didn't you open the door?" I heard no response from him. So once I turned off the stereo, I returned to the bedroom. I walked toward him and shook his body, but no response. His legs dangled off the edge of the bed like he had no intentions of getting up, ever again. I shook him again and again; when I grabbed his right hand, it was as if it had been in an ice box, cold and stiff.

"Luis!" I called out, repeatedly, cried out, "Someone killed you. Someone killed you." My screams were uncontrollable. Yet no tears. Then, my eyes looked and looked around the room. Then, I ran to my room; I did not know what else to think. I sat on the floor near my bed; I closed my eyes, and, in my mind, I saw the rifle, bullet shells, and stuff that was pulled out from the closet. I continued sitting for a bit longer. I was still not crying; I was just scared for a little bit. Eventually, I got enough courage to call my parent's work and informed the office secretary. I told her who I was and what had happened. She notified the emergency departments. In a few minutes, the fire department arrived, and soon after that, the neighbors gathered to see what happened.

At first, I thought someone had killed him. But no, he took his own life. Two strange things happened. The first was before my parents arrived. A phone call came in, and I answered it. The caller was a woman that he had been going out with behind my parents' backs. I yelled at her, "You bitch, you killed my brother."

The second strange thing was after my parents arrived, Mama was destroyed when she got out of the car and found out that one of her sons was dead. Five minutes after that, a priest arrived in an elongated white car with our little brother, Daniel. According to Daniel, he said, that priest he was looking for the street we lived on; Napa, the priest, said that a very desperate young adult had called him at his church asking for help, and when Daniel was walking home, he asked him for directions, and he said to him, "Hop on I'll give you a ride home."

I still don't know if the young adult who called the priest was Luis, but I am convinced and know that God is everywhere, and he sends his messengers, like the priest, like an angel sent by God. Because Mama was destroyed, she needed kind words from a godly man to accept this terrible thing, one of the worst things a mother can go through.

I also do not know why Luis was so determined to do this. The way he looked for Papa's rifle and bullets was like if he was so desperate to leave this world, there were bullet shells all over the floor. Something set him off, and I will never know what it was. Did he have a fight with that woman? Did he tell her he was going to kill himself? At least that was the rumor that we later, the family, heard. Whatever it was, I will never forget that day. That day it is so present in my mind; it is as if it was yesterday. I still ask myself many questions. Maybe if I had stayed with him to go to school together, just maybe he would still be here?

Now, I remember certain moments with Luis and realize he was very depressed. We could not see that then because we were too young and our parents did not know the symptoms. But there were occasions that I was in the car with Luis, that he wanted to run the red lights while driving. I would tell him the light is red, and he would say, "I hate shopping." He would go right through the light; I shut my eyes hoped to be safe. I would avoid riding with my brother if it was possible. I never thought there was anything wrong with him, but after I learned that people suffer from depression and that depression is not prejudiced against anyone. I'm now convinced that Luis needed professional help, but no one noticed that to help him.

Also, Luis suffered a terrible incident when playing flag football while in P.E. when we were going to school in Kerman, and he was an eighth-grader. Another kid landed with his knee on Luis's private area. Due to the severity of the injury, one of his testicles had to be removed. Luis was a different boy after that. He had some counseling. However, I do not think he ever healed correctly in his mind.

He seemed to be okay, but there were strange things he would say to me. Like I thought you were supposed to die, or junior, the devil's nephew, said everyone is going to die, and when we would go to church, he would tell us that he would break into a sweat when being inside the church. Now all this could have been just things he would think to escape what he was feeling; after all, he had gone through severe trauma.

Well, after his death, everyone was pretty shaken up. Mama had to see a doctor due to depression. He prescribed tranquilizers for her to cope with the anxiety. But, after a few weeks, he told her she had to cope with it on her own. Mama pleaded for more, but he was very firm with her and advised her to go window shopping whenever she felt sad.

Mama followed the doctor's advice to the letter. Sooner than later, mom, my sister, and I all became shopaholics. Nothing else eased our sorrows, only trips to the stores.

One time we even tried to smoke our pain away. It was a Saturday afternoon; all the women, on one of the visits to the Fulton Mall, Mama, her sister, my sister, cousin Tita, and me, we bumped into a tobacco company promoting their brand-new Virginia Slims. Well, we all got a sample package, and for two weeks, we sat around the kitchen table thinking of our Luis as we smoked. But Mama's adulthood kicked in and said, "Ya no mas, esto tiene que parar" (this has to stop!). She took all the packages of cigarettes and threw them away. Mama was not about to start a bad habit and let her daughters and niece be dragged into it, either.

I remember when I worked in the convalescent hospital around 1985–1986. All the nurses smoked in the lunchroom, and I wanted so bad to smoke like them. But I would always think of what Mama did that one time when she caught Luis smoking weed. Plus, thanks to this co-worker named Sheila, she took me under her wing. She told me, "No, Chavez, you do not need to learn this. Is a hard habit to kick." What did I tell you about Mama? She has always been a strong and very spectacular woman. She and God always had an angel sent by my side.

On another occasion, when I was thirty years old, I had already had my second daughter, and I got some crazy idea if I could smoke, I could lose weight and drop all the weight I gained from my pregnancy. Well, my two nieces and daughter told me to their grandma (my mama). She called me, very heated, demanded me to stop that nonsense. She did not even care to listen to what I had to say. I was at work, and I could not get a single word in for my defense. She told me that she was my mother and she would tell me what to do until the day she was gone. I never, never, ever, again thought of smoking, ever again!

After Louis's death, I pretty much went to school alone; my cousin Tita use to go with me. But since she was still learning English, she spent most of her school hours at Hamilton School – it was an extension of Fresno High. Plus, she had her own group of friends who always spoke Spanish and enjoyed their company.

During my sophomore year, some of my friends talked about losing their virginity. Others talked about what type of marijuana joints they smoked. I pretty much just heard them and had no clue what to think. I considered myself a virgin since I had never done it all the way. And, there was no way I would even think of smoking marijuana.

I can still remember the day that my mama discovered that Louis was smoking marijuana. It was enough for me to say 'No to Drugs' thank you. In one of my mama's lessons, we were all driving back from her *compadres* home after a day of *carne asada* and playing with the family's relatives. Well, immediately after driving away, Mama got a whiff of that unmistakable odor. She turned back to all of us as we sat quietly in our dad's avocado-colored large car. I kind of had an idea why Mama was so mad. But I knew I had nothing to worry about because I was not the one she was looking at. It was like she knew exactly where the smell came from.

Immediately, after Dad parked the car in our driveway, Mama jumped out and pulled my brother Louis to the side; Papa did not say a word; he let Mama take care of the punishment, and he said to the rest of us to go inside the house, after a while later both Mama and Louis came in the house, Louis had tears in his eyes and was punished for weeks. Mama talked to all of us and warned us if any of us did what Louis had done, she would be very upset, and she would call the police and let them take us into a correctional facility. Drugs were not permitted with her and her children. We had no clue what that was, but yes, we got the idea. Mama knew drugs were bad because that was one of the reasons she decided to move from the neighborhood when we lived in Tio Alberto's house; she saw gangs of young teens, boys, and girls using drugs in the abandoned homes, back in la colony in Mexico. And she was not going to allow any of her children to get drawn into that, which she feared the most. Now that I think about it, I know that Mama wanted to help protect us from the bad by bringing us to the United States; she never thought what sort of things she would confront in this country. But I guess it does not matter where you go in the world. There will always be concerns; human behavior is inevitable. There will always be bad influences and temptations no matter where we go. Mama learned pretty quickly because she began to use her motherly instincts and scared away from my sister and me any acquaintances that she did not receive good vibes from.

In my mind, I knew what could happen to me if I made the wrong choices as Louis did. So, I was careful about what friends to have in Fresno High. There were whites, blacks, punk-rockers, Cholos, Hmongs, and people that looked like me. I used to hang around with two girls name Licha and Tessie. But, for most of the time, I sat under the flag pole, ate my lunch, I would pack a sandwich with my Green

Jalapeno Chile because it just did not taste the same without a bit of spice. I, then, would go to my classes. I was shy to be around boys because they always looked at me like they wanted to eat me. I did not pay attention to whatever comments they made.

"You're the hottest chic here; why don't you party with us?"

They had many other lines to that effect.

I preferred to stay by myself and be sort of distant social.

Going to a big school like Fresno High was hard to get used to. My old school, Kerman, was smaller and had a much closer community, where everyone knew one another. But that change had no effect on my little brother Daniel.

By the time I was a senior, Daniel was a sophomore. Let me tell you everyone knew who Daniel was. He was very popular and had many friends like he does today. Before he started to drive, I drove him and his friends to break dancing competitions. Daniel was a pretty good break dancer. He and his buddies were one of the best groups around Fresno then. So, that was pretty cool. I got to experience this with my brother.

It was also a great way for teens to stay away from drugs and gangs. Because living in the park side, it was not always easy for them to avoid going bad.

Now, I understand why Daniel is how he is; he was always able to make friends and influence others. He knew how to be the center of attention always. I, on the other hand, was always timid and more of a lone wolf. I did have some friends at the beginning of my sophomore year. But, toward the end of my senior year, my life was more about working in the convalescent hospital and hanging around with my boyfriend.

The first friend that I met in my sophomore year was Tessie. She had moved here from Austin, Texas, and she talked differently than me. She was also blonde and very pretty. Her parents both worked office jobs, and the family lived in a nice home. If I recall, it was near West and Shaw. My family, on the other hand, lived in the park side area, across from Roeding Park, and my parents worked in the packing house. The place they lived at was like a townhouse with a community pool. I remember going swimming after school was out. Tessie and I became friends in class. Since we were new to this school, we teamed up and became buddies then and there.

Tessie was not shy. She used to call me 'edge' or 'square'. I wanted to be like her, but there was no way that I could do what she did and get away with it. She liked skipping classes and taking off with other boys riding around, and then she would get dropped off when it was time to go home. I always told her 'No'. Pretty soon, she attracted other friends and began to slip away. I saw less of her around the school campus and in our classes. She soon became popular with some of the football players, the ones that made comments about me being the prettiest, and so on.

Well, Tessie called me when she lost her virginity. She told me she was at this guy's house, his parents had gone out of town, and she had gone, with him, all the way.

All I remember is asking her, "How did it feel? Were you scared?" My curiosity stayed with me, always wondering what it would feel like. I do not remember if she said how it felt. She just sounded a little nervous and confused. From that day forward, I could not stop thinking of my friend's experience with a boy. And after she made new friends, I lost the only friend I had in high school. Actually, I saw her around campus once in a while. Even then, she still called me "Square girl" Tessie was now friends with the popular crowd, with the same guys that would tell me I was the prettiest and finest looking girl in school. Maybe that's what they told every girl? I felt sad that Tessie and I did not hang around together. I used to think it was my fault, like if I was not at all interested in keeping a friend and if I could do what the others were doing, I would then be more accepted.

I did not want to think about that, but the peer pressure was still there. My friend, it turned out, was with several guys before she became the girlfriend of one guy and then stopped going to school altogether. I couldn't understand it though; She was a fast typist, every subject came easy for her, she spoke and read perfect English. "Of course she did; English was her native language." I was a slow typist; my English still sounded broken when I used it, and comprehending what I read was difficult. So, I had to work at it all the time. Unlike me, Tessie was very smart, book smart; that is, I still think of her. I hope she turned her life around; that is what I pray for her always! But before that happened, I can say I had some fun times with my friend.

At the end of my sophomore year, Mama bought me a brown Cutlass Supreme to go to school and to attend my nursing classes. I was so happy. But my papa was not. Mama always did things for us so we would learn not to depend on others. She felt that way because she never learned how to drive, and if we knew how to drive and got a license, we could take her to work and anywhere she needed to go.

Whenever I would catch up with Tessie, I'd take her to my house and then taker her to hers. On one particular day, my mama saw me with my friend Tessie, and I immediately saw the look on my mother's face. It was time for me to take my friend home. The whole way there and back, I was quiet. I knew I would hear an ear full when I got home. Sure enough, my mama was waiting for me outside and scolded me.

"*Lydia ya no quiero que me traigas a esa amiguita a esta casa y no ya no quiero que sea tu amiga!*" She basically said she did not want me bringing my friend to the house and for me to stop hanging around with her. Mama had such a good instinct. I have never had that; she sensed that Tessie was a wild one and trouble girl and soon would influence me too.

Oh my God, what happened? What did my mom see? That was confusing. I had only one friend and could no longer spend time with her. Mama did not understand. I was making good choices. I did not have sex and was not smoking or using drugs, and I wanted to be a nurse. But did I ever tell her how I felt? No, I did not.

I was bored and felt that I should join a sport so that sophomore year I tried out for track-and-field, and I felt great preparing for some track meets. I was running every day after school, up to seven miles a day. It felt terrific. And just about a few weeks before the first track meets, I was told by Mama to quit. Mama saw that I had busted a blood vessel on the back of my knee of my right leg, she panicked. She did not understand that; it was maybe because I did not stretch or warmed upright. She did not want to hear it, so I quit. Well, after that I had nothing to do so I made friends with this senior guy, named Arnold, he was half Mexican half Italian, he was a super nice guy. He asked me to be his girlfriend; I said yes, he would walk me to my classes, and at times, I would give him a ride to his house from school. I never told my parents I had a boyfriend and kept it to myself. And before the school year ended, I ended our relationship because I told him that since the year was over and we would not see each other anymore. Plus, he was a senior. But I actually had another guy in my thoughts. Was this the time I begin to learn the behavior to trap guys and drop them whenever I was tired of them? More like love them and leave them!

It was my next-door neighbor, Chris. He lived with his brother and sister-in-law. I had noticed him before but really did not acknowledge him until the end of my sophomore year. Yes, it really does happen, just like in the movies, meeting the boy next door. He was older, had a job, a car, and dressed nicely.

Since I was in school all day long, we would see mainly in the evening. I would go out to water the plants or wash my car in front of the house. He so happened to be out there too. I had a feeling he liked me, and I was pretty sure I liked him also. This went on for a few months until the early spring of 1985. He had the courage to ask me out; he invited me to go on a drive with him in his brother-in-law's convertible Miata.

I replied right away. "If you want me to go anywhere with you, ask my dad's permission first." I'm pretty sure that shocked him at first. But, if he really wanted me to date him, he had to go through my dad first. I was just sixteen, almost seventeen. What was he thinking? He was like twenty-two or twenty-three. What the heck! No one was thinking, really. But Dad gave me permission to go with him after he lectured us.

Chris was a Chicano, and although his parents were Hispanic, he did not act similar to us. However, he knew very little Spanish, so Dad's vocabulary was a problem for him. But Chris found the words and the courage to ask my papa to let me go on a ride with him.

I still remember how nervous he was; he wore long, checkered shorts that, while he was sitting, made him look like an *indita* when they pull their skirt down to cover their legs. He also wore a pink Le Tigre shirt and moccasin-style shoes with no socks. He also had curly hair that, at that moment, seemed like it curled even more.

Papa told us both in Spanish, *Si tienen mi permiso, pero tienen que ser responsible porque la carne is debil* (yes, you both have my permission, but you both need to be responsible because the body or *carne (meat)* can be feeble).

Chris was pretty confused and asked me why my dad was talking about a piece of meat? Obviously, my papa was referring to our bodies. But I did not know why he used the metaphor for a piece of meat. Well, I guess Dad was onto this guy because, sure enough, our bodies and minds did weaken. Because five to six months later, I lost my virginity to him. And it happened in my own house, in my own room.

My bedroom was located toward the front of the north side of the property, and the window was on the north side of the house, my parents' bedroom was on the south side in between the kitchen and dining room, and Daniel's room was clear down on the same side west of theirs. At night Chris would sneak into my bedroom through the window. The windows in our house were the old style that pushed out to open. Chris would access the entrance through there. This all took place a couple of years after my brother's death, and during that period, my sister was not living with us.

So, you can say I took advantage of my parents' grieving period and vulnerability. I was not getting any attention from my parents and was getting away with my behavior. I was making wrong choices, and my parents were both doing their best to keeping in a roof over our heads. I had no clue what I needed to do, but would you know, Chris did, of course, he did, he had done this before, and he knew exactly what to do to avoid getting me pregnant. Maybe he was smart enough to avoid that because of what Papa had told him. Whatever he was doing, work because I never got pregnant.

As I said, Papa has always had his way of speaking to us. I guess Papa is a thinker, and when he speaks, he speaks with his heart. In the past, I have read some of the songs he used to compose. I must be like Papa because I can sure express myself better when writing than when speaking.

Regards to me losing my virginity, I can't say I completely regret it happened, but I'm not completely happy it happened the way it did; just the fact I betrayed my parents' trust made me feel bad. Especially my papa, what was I thinking? I was dating a guy that was much older had more experienced, and he had no idea what my papa was trying to convey with his metaphor the first day Chris asked me out.

Papa had a way with words, I know. However, that was how he was raised. He only went to third grade, and the rest of his childhood, he concentrated on working to help his younger siblings survive after his mother died and his dad was a total drunk.

There was a time when Luis was still alive when he tried talking to him. Papa tried to use his parenting skills on my brother before he died. He and Mama found out Luis had been having an affair with that older woman, the one that called looking for him, the day of his death. This lady was, in fact, related to their *compadre's* wife; it was her sister. I was not present when Papa reprimanded our brother's actions. I overheard Papa telling Mama that he told Luis, if he needed to be with a woman, he would give him money to pay for a prostitute and lend him his truck. I do not remember what happened after that. But, pretty much, he was supposed to break up with her and move on with his life; this occurred a few days or so prior to his death.

However, he did not obey Papa. Instead, he moved out of the house and into the detached garage. Mama always worried about him. The fact that we lived in a rough *vecindad* (neighborhood) that's why Mama had more reasons to worry. The area we lived in was known and still is known to this day as "parkside" a lot of drug activities, and gangs were already formed around those times.

Mama was concerned for Louis, but Little did she know that her *hijo* was struggling to figure out who he was and if what he felt for this woman was love or lust.

Louis was a very talented young teen. He loved art and was the best GQ dresser way before John F. Kennedy Jr. His favorite performer was Prince and the band Cameo. He adored Bruce Lee movies and was always concerned about his weight. He was about 6 ft tall and never weighed more than 125 lbs, but his arms were muscular, and his stomach was cut like a *lavadero* (washboard).

Although Louis had all these great attributes, he always dealt with negative self-identity issues and alienation. He felt that he would never be able to get a job because when he would apply at any restaurant, the questions always came up.

"What is your Social Security number? Are you a resident?"

Luis felt like the field was the only place he would ever work. So why, exactly, he took his life, we will never know. However, all these things, plus the fact he felt like less of a man since that incident he suffered in jr. high. These pressures were probably enough to set him emotionally off. He felt that his life was over.

It is so important to know your children. Never let them go on thinking that problems and concerns do not have solutions. Understanding that in life, we will all go through heartaches, but with the help of our family, we can get through it, no matter what it is. Like Papa said, "la carne es debil" I finally figured out what he was referring to was about carnality, giving ourselves to sensual pleasures and appetites. Pretty much, our mind is what allows these things to take over us.

My brother had lots of people he could have talked to. Yet, he still felt alone. We still don't know if he was shy, afraid, or just stubborn and thought he would figure it all out on his own. But these were serious problems that needed professional help.

Never think you are alone. Depression, fear, and being confused can lead to fatal consequences. I will always remember my brother as the person he really was. Though he lost himself on this earth, I have faith that God has given his soul the opportunity to be forgiven and has found peace. I want to believe that. I even believe that he has pleaded for us with God; how else can I explain how fortunate my family has been with having great health, jobs, and all the necessary things we need to survive.

Stopped here.

First Time for Everything

Again, you have heard that there is always a first time for everything. Well, in my case, there were many different firsts. Like the first time, I went to school or the first time I was kissed by a boy. But how I truly remember my first innocent kiss. I was seven; Jesus was a cute little boy that lived across the street from the home we were renting of Tio Roberto. In fact, Tio Roberto lived very close to the first home our family purchased here in Fresno.

I also remember my first dreams of becoming a model movie star. Later I had the first dream of having a career as a nurse. So, I went to school to become a Nursing Assistant. The whole junior year, I studied, and by the time I was a senior. I got my first real job in a convalescent hospital. I was so excited. I was living my dream of helping people, taking vital signs, feeding patients, and assisting registered nurses.

During my senior year, I worked eight hours a day up to five days a week. I barely passed all my classes, and I was tired every day. My first class, Government, was at eight in the morning. When you are young, you don't think about how you are going to do something; you just do it. At least, that was how I felt.

There were days when I pulled double shifts and functioned on very little sleep. Thank goodness I was dedicated, and my government teacher called me an 'Italian Monster'. Later, I found out why. He thought that I was as nice looking as Sophia Loren. I guess I knew I was pretty. However, I did not feel I could get by just on good looks. I always worked hard, and I was very responsible. Even before the age of eighteen, which I really did not care much about turning eighteen and becoming an adult, I already felt like an adult a few years before.

For me, it was not important to be pretty; that's what I used to think, but deep inside, I knew guys looked at me differently. Maybe that got to my ego just a bit because I was getting attention from the jock boy from school and other boys that had girlfriends. Around this time, I also had a boyfriend. For some reason, there were just a few that caught my attention. Anyways, some of these guys caught my attention, but I never was daring enough to speak to them. I felt I was beneath them, and plus, they hung around with the popular crowd. I, on the other hand, did not have any friends in school, but I did have friends from work, so I hung around with Tonnie and Sara. Tonnie lived with her father, two brothers, and two younger sisters. Their mother had died a few years before I met her. Sara was bubbly and very pretty and lived with her grandmother. She was as young as Tonnie and me. I was so surprised when she told us that after graduating high school, she and her boyfriend planned to get married.

One time my friend Tonnie invited me to go to a concert. I had no clue what genre of music would be; this was my first concert ever. Thinking back, I know now that my dress attire was a bit skimpy. I wore a blue mini skirt and blacktop with a blue jacket and high heel shoes. Turned out that this concert was rap music and it was loud. The majority of the population there was black. There were also some Chicanos and a few whites. Well, Tonnie took the liberty to invite some guys sitting around us to go with us to a house party, and not only that, she even told them where we worked. I was just following my friend's lead. But I was uncomfortable with this because I did not tell Mama where I was going. The last time I asked her for permission to go with my friends to a bridal shower at a cabin, she did not let me go. So, this time I pretty much just lied to her and told her I was working a double shift because work was the only place she would let me go.

Anyway, I didn't know if Tonnie knew any of these guys or not. But, the next day, when our shifts ended, around 11pm, the two guys from the concert, there they were, outside near our cars, waiting for us. One of them was very persistent with me. Every time I turned there, he was. He was not a bad looking black guy. I was sure Tonnie felt bad for me; she didn't mean to bring that on to me. I can't blame her, I should have filed a police report, but I did not know that what he was doing was borderline stocking.

My boyfriend Chris and I were not seeing each other as much; he was older and would hang around with his buddies drinking and doing other things. So, this new friend was paying a lot of attention to me. He invited me to his house. This was the first time I went to the West Side, which is where he and his family lived. As a matter of fact, this was the first time I ever met and socialized with a black family, period. He took me around to meet family and had the chance to meet his grandmother. He introduced me to his barber, there at his neighborhood barbershop, I waited for him while he got a hair trim. Most of the barbers at the barbershop were older men, but they would not keep their eyes off me. They cracked up a whole lot, made comments that sounded like this "Whoa, you go, brother," and other funny gestures. I felt uncomfortable; they were speaking English but could not comprehend what they were really saying. I also got to meet other of his friends. They were nice and funny too. At the time, I felt a little uncomfortable because he seemed to be very careless; the way he would talk and act was different from what I was using. We came from two different worlds, but it did not seem to affect him at all. I, on the other hand, could not see past his color and mine. He always carried on telling me how beautiful I was, and his playful ways were liberal. He seemed to come from money. He drove a nice car, but there was something about him that I could not figure out. He told me that he came from the Los Angeles area. I knew where that was, as I had passed through there when we first arrived from Mexico. As a matter of fact, he said to me, "My mom lives in LA and works for IBM." I had no idea who or what that was. But I was not sure why he lived in Fresno with "auntie," as he would say, and uncle. All I know is that he lived near the Chandler Airport. I had never been in that neighborhood before, and to this day, I could not remember where he lived. It was like a blur, like if that never really happened.

Every time I thought he would not look for me, I turned around, and he would be there right behind me, everywhere, school, and work. After all that, I gave myself to him. He was so persistent. And of course, I did not think of protection, what? No! I was so stupid. I never thought I would have sex with anyone else other than my boyfriend, Chris, and he made sure that I did not get pregnant. I assumed Kevin would do the same thing. So, no, with this new fling, I was not using protection; oh my! How did I not get pregnant? No one knows, I guess. I can say I was lucky because Kevin and I were very much sexually active. I would see Kevin during my lunch breaks. He was just having fun, and he was kind of crazy. I was always nervous around him because I did not know what to expect from him. He was different than other boyfriends I've had. But Kevin was the complete opposite. He would all of suddenly appear in front of me, or he would sometimes call me at home and put his mom on the phone. I never knew what to expect from him.

One night he came to my house, uninvited, and I tried to introduce him to my family. My papa did not say a word. He just stood up and walked past him. I right away knew Papa was mad at me. Papa went to his room and did not come out the rest of the night. The next day I heard it from Papa. He used to be the least to discipline between him and Mama. But that day, he talked to me very harshly. Usually, Papa said very few words to us, but when he felt uncomfortable or felt he needed to say something and be heard, we heard him loud and clear. Papa kept telling me this boy was bad company, telling me to stay away as far as possible. I never asked him why he was against me seeing Kevin or why he did not want to meet him. He did not care how I felt. I felt dad was rude and, yes, I did feel bad and embarrassed, that did not matter, he said to me the words, No Quiero, I do not want to know or hear you are with that guy. All I could imagine that Papa may be did not get a good impression of Kevin or that he felt I should only interact with people of my own race. I did not have a strong relationship with Kevin, nor did I feel that not seeing him would break my heart. I was just puzzled as to why my father behaved that way toward him.

The next time I heard from Kevin was just to tell him that my father did not want me to see him, and pretty much he got the idea that Papa did not care for him. I never heard from him again.

Since 4th grade, I pretty much spent the rest of my elementary, junior, and high school years learning English and trying to understand and speak it correctly. I did not pay much attention to current events. I now know why? Because I did not know all about the days of segregation. And also, I lived in Mexico through the whole Civil Rights Movement until I got to college in January 2009. Until then, I learned more of this country's history and even learned more of Mexico's history. I was much too young when I was brought here from Mexico, and when you do not practice it, you lose it. I'm not ashamed of sharing this because I'm happy that I finally got the opportunity to learn it. I can't really say that my parents were prejudice because of the way they reacted back then. What I can say is that they did not know history. People from Mexico, at least back at the time when we lived there, it was only one race. We did not mix with other races at the time. So, we did not know that there were any differences in cultures. We were all the same. So, I thought we were living in Mexico; I felt there was no prejudice, no racism. I was wrong. Mexico their traditions, cultures; after all, we are all equal, right? I must admit I was closed-minded like my parents. But, since I'd been studying, I have changed my way of thinking and see life with much more open eyes. I choose to say whether I agree or disagree, but not until I first analyze the facts and make an unbiased decision. I give everyone the benefit of the doubt.

Back when I was in high school, soon it was time to concentrate on graduating from high school, but I was not too sure I was going to graduate. My government class was my first class in the morning, and going to bed late every night after working. I could never seem to concentrate, never managed to keep my eyes open, while Mr. Tevriz lectured and showed us movies about politics and historical cases. So, I asked Mr. Tevriz if I was passing his class. I was scared because I knew I was not doing well because all my test scores were pretty low. Everything the teacher talked about was so confusing to me. Imagine English as a second language. I could barely remember Mexico's history, but well, he answered.

"Yes! Why shouldn't I pass you? You are here every day even though you fall to sleep, not like some of the lazy students in your row that don't even show up to class. Plus, it would be a shame to flunk a young Sophia Loren, the Italian Monster."

I later found out why he called me that. He wanted to express to me that I looked like Sophia Loren. I guess I disappointed my government teacher because I never became a hot movie star as he thought. I wish, though, I would have known who Ms. Loren really was because maybe I'd want to be like her. She is one of the most beautiful women I had ever seen. The day I graduated when he handed me my diploma. He said, "Let me know when your first movie is out."

I was happy I graduated. But there are two things I regret not doing. One was not going to Grad Night and taking the senior trip to Hawaii. I remember my homeroom teacher making announcements.

"Make your deposit for the grand night and a trip to Hawaii."

I had the money for both things since I was working full-time. I gave some money to my mama and the rest you can say I spent. But now that I think about it, I don't think my mama would have allowed me to go to Hawaii, maybe to Disneyland. Anyhow, I did not even bother to ask her. I convinced myself that the convalescent hospital needed me. Who would feed my patients? Who would get them out of bed? Especially my patient Larry, he was the most adorable 40-year-old patient. He was born mentally ill, could not walk, talk, and lived all his life in a bed. I would bathe him, change him and feed him. I always made sure he was out of bed and put into a recliner chair, and looked out his window. I thought about Larry. I knew how hard it was when someone called in sick, how short-staffed we would be, and that was something I did not want to cause. I was responsible; you could say that. But I did not stop to think that you are only young once and graduate from high school once in your lifetime.

I remember that my sister Angela went to her Grad-Nite, and she looked so beautiful in her Grad-Nite picture. A couple of years later, after I graduated, my youngest brother, Daniel, also went. Of course, he had a blast. I saw his pictures. He saw Blondie in concert. Imagine how I felt. I really regretted not going. I missed out!

The next thing to do was think about college. But really, nobody was pushing me. I was working, paying bills, plus I had no idea how to enroll in college. I was also the greatest person to talk myself out of things. I was still illegal, and without a permanent card, I would not be allowed in college, at least that is what I used to think. I would say to myself if I can work for a year or two, I can later take night classes and get my License in Vocational Nursing, and eventually continue my education to receive my Degree as a Register Nurse.

None of those plans were ever reached, but fortunately, I always had faith that things would change for people like many other undocumented people and me.

I enjoyed working, but I was always inspired to do better. After graduating, all I did was work, work, and work. Even though I did not do too much, other than hanging around with Chris, my boyfriend, during my days off. I also enjoyed going to the gym. I was a member of the well-known 'Four Walls' back in the late 1980s. I still have a workout tank top shirt that I purchased from them with the name on it. I enjoyed working out every day, aerobics was my favorite, and after a great workout, I would relax in the sauna for thirty minutes. But working out was out of the question when I was working in Beverly Manor, which was the convalescent hospital I worked in. I was always tired because whenever another employee would ask me to cover their shift on my days off, I could not say no; whenever the personnel department would call me to go on and cover a shift, I could not say no. Whenever I was on my regular shift, and someone would not show up or call in sick I was asked to cover, I would not say no. I would work double shifts, sometimes work two weeks straight without a day off. My mother instills in each of her children good working ethics, and turning away work hours was unheard of in our house. After all, that is the reason we came to America. The promised land, where dreams do come true, you just must work hard.

As I said, I love my job and enjoyed it, but sometimes I felt like a circus elephant with a chain on his ankle, unable to run away.

Then a job landed on my lap. I got hired to be an assistant for a chiropractic office. I held two jobs for the short term. I worked at Beverly Manor working a graveyard shift, and I worked three days a week with my new job. I did this for three months; toward the end of the year, I was offered to work full-time and take over the duties as an office manager. Fall came around, and I no longer worked in the convalescent hospital. I was now an office manager and making a great salary. School or College was nowhere near my thoughts. I lived it up: boyfriend, new car, and money. That's all I need, right? No, not really. I was going about it all wrong!

I was about eighteen years old. Eighteen! The age said it all.

I especially thought about it when my daughters came into that age. I know times change, and we, my siblings and me, our parents were different; they were hard on us. They were making sacrifices, and I can imagine they were also feeling scared of us taking the wrong paths or making wrong choices. They had lost one son, and they were going to do whatever to keep us on the right path. I'm convinced that, at that age, I had no business having a boyfriend, especially since he was about four years older. He drank, he smoked weed, and he had different morals. I was not thinking! I guess I was just happy to be loved and be like and follow all of my peers. The only thing that I'm proud of through all this is that I never drank or used any type of drugs. I guess I knew well what would happen to me. Our mama and Papa always warned us of the dangers of drugs and gangs.

During the time I had this boyfriend, I never told Mama I was sexually active. Who was I kidding? She knew. But she never sat down to talk to me. Maybe she was embarrassed? Maybe she did not want to know? Maybe she was just praying so hard for me not to get pregnant. Well! Her prayers were answered. Because I had no clue about contraceptives. I was naive, stupid, and a total Idiot! What would I have done if I'd come up pregnant! I had no plans. I was just so young; I was no different than my friend from high school, Tessie; if she could only see me, I was no longer a "Square."

My boyfriend's family was what you would call Chicanos. His parents spoke Spanish, but the children preferred to speak English. Their way of cooking was also different, and even the way they celebrated the holidays. After a while, I started to withdraw from my boyfriend. There were times that his family made me feel like I was an idiot. It's like if I had some letters written across my forehead *Mexicana*. I tried not to let that bother me too much. But, little by little, I began to become less interested in him. Well, I never talked with my parents about what I was thinking. I always worked out my problems on my own, and as long as I was giving my mama money on a monthly basis, I thought I was a good daughter. During my senior year, our family achieved the American dream. Papa received a worker's compensation settlement due to an injury; he gave my mama and sister Angela the money to buy a home. At first he was reluctant to, but Mama and my sister finally convinced him. You see, my papa always thought that since we were illegally in the country, the government could send us back to Mexico anytime take all we had earned. All our hard-earned accomplishments would have been for nothing. My mama and sister did not listen. I'm very glad they were persistent with Papa putting in some of his settlement money for the purchase of our first new home. Papa was never thinking of the future, he was only thinking of living one day at a time, but Mama had a vision.

My older sister, Angela, has always been like our mama. She planned ahead and always took care of her money well. So the money I gave to Mama helped make the mortgage payment or covered other expenses.

Papa's idea was that he gave us sufficient money to buy the home. He was not going to throw his money into a monthly payment. He always felt it was a waste of money, but he lived there pretty much for free. He was such a hard-headed man, like he still is today, except that he is older and more stubborn. I can't stay mad at Papa; he did his best, never left us to starve in Mexico, and now that he is older, he has nobody else but his children to care for him. I do not hold any resentments toward him. I wish every day for one million dollars to give him a better life in his golden years.

I was pretty much doing what Mama said. We always supported her. She knew what to do. After all, we were in America thanks to her struggles. I wish I can give her all the happiness in the world because she deserves it all!

Well, after being with my boyfriend for almost two and half years, I sought out my culture and started listening to Mexican music and going to the dances at the Rainbow Ballroom. It was different. People were having fun, and the girls and guys my age enjoyed dancing and meeting new friends. Soon my cousin Tita and I made new friends. Since cousin Tita lived with us, she and I got along really well. We were the same age. Our birthdays were a few days apart from one another. We actually acted very similar except that she spoke less English than me, and she did not need to worry about exercising as I did. She had a fast metabolism; unlike me, I had to watch what I ate, diet all the time, and exercise.

Together, Tita and I got to meet many famous group members of music groups like *Los Tigres Del Norte, Los Muecas, Los Bukis*, and *Los Jonics*. It was pretty cool; you could say we were groupies in a sense, but not really because we did not engage in any sexual activity with them. We just took pictures, and that was pretty much all.

Doing this sort of helped me see things from a different perspective. I was now talking more Spanish, listening to Spanish music and of course, started to meet other young people that were more like me, working hard and were illegally in the United States too. My favorite dance was when we saw *Los Bukis* live at the Fresno Fair Dance hall, on the side of Butler. I never saw a live band, and two of my cousins were so excited because that was their favorite band. I, on the other hand, had no clue who they were. So I wore a low-cut black dress with a gold zipper all the way down the front and black high heels. The crowd was unbelievable, it was loud, and everyone was chanting the band members names. I separated from my cousin, and I ended up pretty close to the front of the stage. As soon as the band came out, the crowd started to push forward. On one occasion, I felt like if I was grabbed from behind. I turned around and slapped the guy behind me.

I yelled at him, "Why are you grabbing my ass?"

He said, "No, it was not me."

"Oh well, since he was the closest, he paid the price."

Meanwhile, the crowd got pretty out of control. About half an hour into the concert, I asked the guy I slapped to help me get on the stage because I wanted out of the crowd, so he does. I was now on the stage, and the singer *(El Buki)* thinks I'm coming up to kiss him. So, he comes to me and hugs me, and that is how I meet *(El Buki)* Marco Antonio Solis. At the same time, my cousins were all wondering where I was, and they got concerned because I alone and lost. However, when they saw me on stage, they no longer felt sorry for me. I also got to meet the rest of the band members, like *El Chivo* and Pedro; they were the most popular. I even got an invitation from Pedro to see him in his hotel room. Which, at that time, they stayed in the Hilton downtown. I declined his invitation, of course. But I had a picture taken with him and asked for his autograph instead. I wish I still had that picture, but I do not know where it stayed; after all, I have moved around a lot!

I have to say my fun lasted a short time. I did what I always wanted. I got to make commercials, and someone advised me to run as a candidate, to be a queen of the 15 September festivities.

I did do it, but unfortunately, I did not win, although I got to meet more important people, people that were in the media and were helping me achieve my long-gone dreams. The dreams I gave up on, such as becoming a model and getting into acting. I got started by doing voice-over commercials, and soon, I was receiving more requests from other vendors like attorney's offices and stores like Save Mart. During this time, I was about twenty years old, and I had no boyfriend because I broke up with Chris. So, I was pretty much meeting friends and going on dates. This was the best time of my young adult life. Well, after these things got to be better for everyone like me, who was undocumented and had not been to Mexico for many years. Until the day came when for all undocumented persons and families across the country in the U.S.A., their prayers were answered. In 1986, the amnesty law was passed.

Everybody, I mean everybody, applied for the *micas*, the green cards, thank you, Jimmy Carter and Ronald Reagan. I thank Jimmy Carter because he was a great president that was always looking out for the migrant workers. *Viva America! And Viva Mexico!* Here comes all your lost *hijos* (children) to visit, celebrate and move back. Well, the application would take a few months before we could go out. For some people, it processed faster; others took longer. Some people went to visit, and some people did move back, but not our family. We had a house of our own. Angela and Mama paid the mortgage, and I contributed for miscellaneous. My brother Daniel did the right thing. He chose to get an education. From all the children, he always knew what he wanted. When he was 15 years old, he went to work with Papa in the fields.

On the second day of fieldwork, he said to Papa, "I'm not doing this, Dad. I'm going to study."

Papa said, "Good for you. That's what I wanted to hear."

Daniel walked out of the field row and told Papa, "Keep the money; I don't want it."

Daniel was about seven years old when we came from Mexico. Due to his age, he started school from the beginning, kindergarten. So, for him, it was a lot easier to adjust to the American ways. Maybe that was so, but really, Daniel always had stronger ambitions than all of us. He wanted to go far. His dreams were a lot more visual than mine. He always did what he wished for. He went to college, and by the time he went to Fresno State, we were legally in this country.

The first Christmas that I was able to cross the border legally in and out was December 30 1987. Well, not really Christmas, more like New Year's. This is also the first time I drank alcohol.

As I said earlier, there is a first time for everything, well for me, once was enough with Vodka. This is why I do not like to drink it. I still remember how badly sick I got. It is on my top ten list of the worst hangovers I ever experienced in my life. But that is not in the number one spot. But, that same night, which was New Year's Eve, I met Joey, my cousin Pita's cousin; oh wow! He liked me, and I liked him. Before I started drinking, my aunt and uncle invited me to my aunt's in-law's house. It was a tradition that at midnight everyone gathered and gave each other a New Year's hug. I was all for traditions. Since we were away for so long, unable to visit, this sounded great. As soon as we arrived at my aunt Lidia's family's house, we walked into the house and heard Spanish rock music playing from a jukebox. There were young kids dancing having a good all time. I walked in a sort of shy but yet ready to celebrate. Everyone in the house begins to say, "Feliz Ano Nuevo!" (Happy new year!) everyone was hugging each other. It felt great, like the "Old days!" Suddenly, I was asked by this handsome guy to dance. He said to me, "Lidia? Hola! Soy Joey." (I'm Joey.) I already knew who he was because my Aunt Lidia and her husband, Tio Roberto, had already informed me all about him. Well, let's just say they were playing cupid. When Joey asked me to dance, I said yes to him; he then asked me if I remember who he was. He said I remember you when you were about eight years old, which was when I met him at Pita's house at the Pina Market. Yes, this was Joey; it was the same guy that I was walking next to when cousin Eddie suffered a cracked on his skull because he was making fun of me with him. How was I to know that fourteen years later, we would meet and fall in love?

Then our uncles were ready to head back to our family's party at my Uncle Jose's house. The unthinkable happened; never did Joey's family ever visited my grandmother's house, much less my tio's next door, my mama Nita. One of his daughters had a crush on this Joey guy, but nothing more than that. He was her age, and they were classmates all the way through high school. So, she saw him every day. And here comes this *pocha* from California and sweeps his heart away from her and any other young girls who had their eyes set on him.

That same night he asked me to dance for New Year's Day; I said 'no', because he was a bit shorter than me. And I was not interested at first, a little bit after that he and his brother left back to their house. Then my cousin came up to me and told me, "You took him from me. Of course, he takes one look at you *y lo hipnotisas*." She said I hypnotized him. Then, she confessed to me that she always liked him, but he did not return her feelings. I did not know what to say. I told her not to worry. It was not what she was thinking. But the next day I found out she had a boyfriend. And, after my hangover left, I was ready to go after this prey, like a hawk. I sought him out and found him even more interesting. In my eyes, he was mine, and there was nothing that could be done.

The day before returning to California, we exchanged phone numbers. After all, my aunt Lidia and his uncle Roberto were hoping that we would get to know each other. He wanted us to meet and even told him that I was going to be at the New Year's dance.

My aunt and her husband failed to tell me that they were trying to set us up. I, of course, was not looking for a relationship. I was dating a guy back at home, but nothing serious. Miguel was his name. He lived in the Coalinga Area during the year of 1988 and 1990.

Actually, when I returned home to Fresno, I spoke with Miguel over the phone – he asked me how was my vacation in Mexico. I actually used the wrong word in Spanish instead of saying that I had met a guy in Mexico and that I was interested in him. I said I was engaged (estoy comprometida). I really do not know what I was really trying to tell him. I just knew that Miguel was just enjoying my company. Visiting me in in Fresno, going out to dances at the Rainbow Ball Room, it was more like a nice friendly relationship, and we had things in common. He liked me. Loved Juan Gabriel, the singer. I knew he had a girlfriend from Salinas, California, and we were just that, friends.

According to him, after I told him I was engaged, he turned around and asked his girlfriend to marry him.

After a short holiday stay in Mexico, my family and I left San Luis to return to Fresno, California. Nine hours later, we arrived home, and one hour after that, the phone rang, guess who? Mom tells me it is Joey. After saying hello, and catching my breath for the excitement of hearing his voice again, he asked me if I would be his date for his graduation dance from the University of Mexicali, which would take place in February; I said yes, of course. He phoned me from his workplace almost every other day. It was like a fairy tale. He was so polite; I was so excited. For some reason, the way he spoke to me sounded so romantic. For the next month and a half, I made plans for the upcoming trip back to Mexico. I did not know what to expect. I had never been to graduation from a university, nor any kind of graduations in Mexico. I was uncertain what would take place. There would be a first special mass following the graduation, and that evening, there would be a special ball for them with friends and family.

The day came on February 8 1988, when Mama and I went to Mexico. I took one week of vacation time from my job, especially for his graduation. I drove in my 1987 Pontiac Firebird. My employer heard rumors that I started to date a guy from Mexico. My boss was older and never interfered in my personal life. But, on this occasion, he did.

He felt threatened and started to think I might get serious with this guy and move away. I was very good at my job as a Chiropractic Manager. I sent out billing invoices to workers compensation, private and automobile insurances. I was pretty successful in collections and billing. My employer's accounts receivable was in great standing, so the last person he wanted to lose was me.

So he asked his golf partner to invite me out. He was supposedly a professional golf player, he was around twenty-two years of age and was very tall, his name was Raul. He seemed to be very respectful and attentive; after meeting him, Raul's first words were, "Do you want to go play golf?"

I had never played golf in my life, and I had no clue that he was just starting a conversation. I simply said, "No."

I did not catch on fast; my boss knew exactly what he was doing. He was just trying to introduce me to new friends around my area.

I now understand that he cared for me as well as his business. My boss said he would never interfere in my personal life.

Joey and I continued our relationship from a long distance. He would call me on Sundays and sometimes during the week.

Joey and I had a perfect second-time meeting. It was the month of romance; valentine's day was near. His graduation, mass, and dance were on Friday, February 12, 1988. Actually, I was only like his date. I wore a black laced strapless dress. I looked very stunning, the first time wearing a strapless dress. I was always self-conscious of exposing my chest, but that night I felt at ease. And that night, during his graduation dance, he asked me to be his girlfriend. He said I know you live far away, but we can manage to communicate by phone, letters, and to visit each other. I said yes, and from there on, our relationship continued in a long-distance way.

Joey and I would see each other whenever I would drive nine hours to see him. Whenever we would see each other, we would go dancing, watch movies, just enjoyed each other's company. He was a gentleman; he respected me. As time passed, he made comments about marriage because there were many times we were alone and came close to having sex, but he knew how to control his sensual appetite; he said he wanted our one day to be special. He wanted to get married, but he always made it clear that his career came first. He was now an engineer and was going to get his master's and go for his Doctorate. In my mind, everything sounded great while I was there. But as soon as I was in Fresno, I was lonely. Imagine beautiful, young, and just waiting for my boyfriend's phone calls. But something else was going on in my mind. I think subconsciously I felt that I did not deserve Joey. I love the way he was and felt it was meant to be; although I was ashamed of who I was, I did not represent that innocent young woman that a fine young man like him typically got married in a white gown with her parents taking her to the alter. I pretty much knew he was thinking I was still a virgin, as that's how he assumed it. Also, he always promised to visit me, he never did. But that was beside the point. I was, more than anything, ashamed to confess to him that I was not who he thought I was.

One day my cousin Tita and I met a guy at our job, the chiropractic office. Since I was the office manager, I hired my cousin and pretty much my best friend to work with me. Well, this guy, his name is Martin. He was around our age, nice and pleasing to talk to. He invited us to have a drink at a bar (Aldos). We were twenty-one years by then. When he asked us if we had boyfriends, I said, "Yes, he lives in Mexico." Then, I talked about him, how smart and nice he was.

He said to me, "*Amor de lejos es amor de Pendejos*," meaning that a faraway love is a lost love in a sense.

That day I realized, why is it that I had to make all the effort to visit him and he didn't visit me. I was always driving 8–9 hours to see him. Well, Martin's words were like a bomb. "Boom!" I set off, I started to go out, dances on the weekends, but still waiting for my boyfriend's long-distance calls. I was like Shakira's song, She-Wolf. During the week, I was a girlfriend, and during the weekend, I was out prowling. My prowling did not go for too long because apparently, I was someone else's prey.

I meet a smooth operator that swept me off my feet. It happened. I let that person come between Joey and me. I did not speak to him or wait for his phone calls. He was long-distance and, like they say, "What you don't know won't hurt you."

The last day I saw him was in May 1989. It was my mama Nita's birthday party. He was working overtime and did not make the party until late. By then, I did not want to see him. I acted like I was asleep, and I returned to Fresno, wrote a letter to him that it was over. I was not even honest with him; I told him that I was going to get me a career and that I would not have time to see him anymore. I broke his heart, we were supposed to baptize his uncle's baby, and I did not show. Later his mom gave him my letter, my cowardly breakup letter. (Nowadays, cowardly people like me break up through emails, text messages, or through any other social network there is.) Even though I was done with this relationship, I really did not let it go. I was not happy with what I did, but what was done was done; there was no going back. I found out a few years later that he had a girl pregnant, and he had a baby that was about one year old, but this was much after he found out I was getting married.

In September of the same year, I got engaged to the guy that swept me off my feet. Florencio was an Italian cook at a local Italian restaurant, divorced, had a son, and he lived with his brother. His brother and his wife lived three houses away from our house on Dayton Ave. I was twenty-one years of age and thought that the world was all mine.

Mama was not happy at all; with my choice, she was right to feel that way. She wanted the best for me; she felt Joey was the best. Instead, I picked a man that had already lived a married life and experienced things I hadn't. Mama would ask us where in the world did we meet these guys? Tita was dating Florencio's nephew, who also worked as a cook at the same restaurant. I understand what Mama was trying to help me realize, although she did could not because I had made up my mind that Florencio was the man that I would spend the rest of our lives together.

A few months before our wedding, I was contacted by the director of the local Univision Chanel 21, who came to me with an idea. He said he and a group of programmers had come up with a morning show to be aired on a daily basis. And he thought of me as the perfect candidate for this show. I had met Jesus Gonzalez and a few other employees from this Channel network, and they had given me an opportunity to make my dreams come true. Was this my break? Well, maybe not, or I was just too stupid to see it. I told Jesus I had just become engaged and was dedicating my time to my marriage. The name of the program is Arriba Valle Central. My fiancé and I did not talk enough on this subject; it was more that he made a choice for me because he did not approve of me exhibit myself on cameras and shows. My break what I always wanted and I chose marriage?

Well, for those who know what morning show I'm referring to, I do not have to tell you that currently, after all these years later, this show is still going strong, and the same spokesperson is still there. Maybe it would have been me, maybe not. Regardless, I did not even try; I just stood there and let my fiancé decide for me. If I could go back into the past, I would tell that girl (myself) off; I would!

Mama knew it all along. She only wanted the best for me, but my head was in the clouds. On the day of the wedding, Mama could not stop crying; she had the saddest face. It seemed like instead of a wedding, she was at a funeral; maybe she was, mine. My dream to marry in a white dress and have a great ball like in the Fairy tales was finally coming true. The wedding was set for February 17, 1990; the months went fast. Then it was January, and Florencio and I were becoming so much more familiar with each other that we got a bit too close; a few days before the wedding, I found out that I was one month pregnant. I was too embarrassed to confess to my *familia*. So I did not tell anyone, except for the groom.

How could I tell my parents that I was not a virgin and that their daughter was expecting a baby; one month before the wedding! I was caught up in this dream of wearing a white gown, and soon my dream would come true. I thought that finally, my wish had finally arrived, my prince charming, he would love me forever, we would both work hard, buy a home and live forever happy.

Now that I look back and think what the hell was wrong with me. I had no reason to get married in a white gown; I had not a single piece of purity. I had lost my purity since I was six years old and lost my virginity by the time I was fourteen when my first boyfriend fondled my body, then later let a twenty-two-year-old guy enter my body. And even after Chris, I continued that reckless behavior. Mama was blaming my fiancé, but really it was my fault for rushing into things. Maybe deep down inside, I felt Florencio was the best that I deserved because no other young man would love me the way I was. I was so messed up! By the time I got to the alter, my white gown was so tainted that only God could see it. Who was I trying to fool! God tried to talk to me, but I did not hear him. He knew that the day would come that I would see everything. I was only fooling myself. I had destroyed my castle way before I begin to build it.

Well, regardless of all that drama that I had going on in my head, but was in denial to admit it. The wedding and reception were very nice; Florencio and I worked very hard to make sure it was; his brother, my family, and friends helped too. After our wedding, the months flew, and my stomach grew, too, and what do you know, I'm pregnant. I gave birth to a *bella nena*, Victoria, named after The

Victorian Era. One thing was for sure holding my newly born, 7.5-pound baby girl close to my heart was the most wonderful thing I ever experienced. "Thank you, God, you are so powerful."

Being a mother was the greatest blessing I could ever ask for, but it seemed like I was feeling this joy all alone. Florencio wished for a boy, and he didn't act like a loving husband and dad. Since it was a girl, he had no part of it. I was starting to feel I was in this all alone. His attitude toward Victoria was not acceptable. He was not taking care of her. Around the same time, my sister Angela gave birth to my niece Missy. I would see how her dad adored his little girl, compared to how Florencio would react with our little one.

I was back to work, and Mama would take care of Victoria for me while both Florencio and I worked. There was a time that Victoria and Missy had to be taken to daycare when Mama's work scheduled changed from pm to am shift. Still, she and Angela would pick up the girls after they came from work. Their workday would end a few hours earlier than mine since I started later than them.

Florencio sometimes would be home when Victoria was home, but Mama would be the one to look out for her and feed her instead of her dad. Mama told me that he would not even make an effort to help her or acknowledge our daughter. I begin to notice this behavior from him. It was as if we did not exist to him. I felt rejected as much as my little baby girl. Every day Victoria grew and would be cuter and cuter. But it was like if we were invisible to him.

One day I came to visit the restaurant; he was a cook at the DiCicco's Italian Restaurant, one of the original locations on Blackstone and Clinton area, presently that location is closed. So on this particular day I walked in, and he did not see me walk in, he was on the phone taking an order, on the counter, when I was leaning, I saw a pad that had his writing, and it had numerous times, Alicia, Alicia, Alicia, Alicia. That was his first love, his ex-wife, which by the way, was married. My daughter and I were just people to him. I understand now that he was in love but not with me. I cannot blame him because I was not in love either; back then, I do not think I knew the definition of love between a man and a woman. When I saw that, I wanted to run out and cry, and maldesir (curse) that name. However, I could not, since that same name is also my mama's. I understood it was not his ex-wife's fault or his son's if he loves them more than me and my daughter I was not going to be in his way and were not to be treated less, that I made sure.

So soon after speaking to my mom and my family. I decided to tell my husband I wanted a divorce. I filed, and my family supported me said that I had to do whatever I felt was right for my daughter and me.

It was tough when it came to breaking off relationships. What it would be to go through the battle of a divorce. For Florencio, this would be his second time. Although when I told him he really did not put up a fight, he simply said, "*Ni modo*" (whatever). I felt guilty that he would have to return to live with his family or look for a place to stay after our separation, so I felt compelled to help him. I offered him money so he can get back on his feet. I, on the other hand, decided to move away and deal with it in my own way.

I quit my job and left for Mexico, all the way to San Luis Sonora, to see if I could pick up the pieces of the heart I broke a few years back. I was not telling anybody those were my thoughts, but that was my whole plan. Maybe now Joey would be okay since I was now free from the person I left him for, and since things did not plan out, maybe just maybe things would be the way they were.

What was I thinking? That's the whole thing I was not thinking. It was no longer about me; it was about Victoria, my daughter, who, at this most crucial time of her life, needed to be around her family, her cousins, including her dad. But instead, I was so selfish. Thinking I can just show up in front of Joey, and in a heartbeat, he would take me back.

Well, that could not get any worst; I was humiliated by Joey pretty much in his intellectual way of speaking. He said to me; this will never be; what we had before will never happen. He was telling me in an implying sort of way, but did I get the idea? No, no, no, I still insisted. I was thinking with my ego, not me. Why would he not want me? I left him. I broke his heart. I felt like Julia Roberts, in My Best Friend's Wedding, chasing after him, and nobody was chasing me.

Later I realized that there were more fish in the sea. And, I had the greatest time in San Luis. I was exercising; I had lost all my baby fat. I was clubbing with my cousin Ana Maria. It was the greatest time; I was not seeing anyone. I was healing from my divorce. At the same time, being rejected by the boyfriend, I so cowardly dumped. What was I thinking?

But during the whole time I was in San Luis, I had a great time getting to know my mama Nita; she told me stories of her past, how her husband took her at the age of fourteen years old, and how we could have been a rich family if only she would have accepted an inheritance from her father. My great-grandfather, her dad, was from a wealthy family in Michoacan, one of the states of Mexico, which by the way, we were told that his parents took place in defending their rights against the times of Purfurio Diaz. Mama Nita's Mom (Mama Cuca) met him when they were both fighting in the Mexican Revolution. My great-grandmother was an Adelita. That was what my grandmother said. I bonded with Mama Nita in the most beautiful way. I couldn't even feel the stress I was going through because I tried many times to get a job and in Yuma, Arizona. Besides, when I was younger in my elementary years, I never felt as discriminated as I did when I was searching for a job. I never got called back for one single interview. My savings were depleted, so I had to go to plan B, which was to sell *tortas* during the baseball games at La Guinitas in San Luis. My tio Robert, Tia Lidia's husband, was in charge of an AAA baseball team. There were games at least two times per week and two games on the weekends.

I made good money. However, there were only so many *tortas* I could make. I was getting tired and bored, so I started to apply for jobs in Mexico. I said if the gringos don't want me, maybe the advantage of my second language will benefit me here. I went on a job hunt, one, in particular, was a new airline coming into Mexicali, and they were looking for bilingual applicants for various positions. I applied among four hundred other applicants; I spent a whole day waiting to be interviewed. I made it! After two interviews, I was told to wait for the final call. After two days I got the call from the head of the Personnel department.

The name of the airline was something Aero Paz; I do not recall the full name. But, yes, he tells me I'm hired as a supervisor of a department. As he is telling me, it was of great joy. But just knowing that amongst four hundred applicants, I made it; I felt that I was taking something from a person who might have prepared for years to get this job. I knew that if I returned to California, I could get a job. I was qualified to work in any doctor's office, being bilingual and highly qualified in that field. California was my home. I no longer lived in Mexico. So, I said thank you to this nice gentleman and declined the job offer. I hope the person that got the position was as happy as I was. Although I was not quite ready to return home, the time finally came around.

In September 1992, my mama came to San Luis for one of the cousins '*quinceanera*'. This was when Mama became concerned about Victoria and me. I was dieting like a nut and begin to get dizzy spells. I was on a diet, eating, Ramen noodles, red skin chicharrones, clamato juice with lemon, and drinking lots and lots of water. Plus, I was running twice a day and doing step aerobics. Regardless, nothing was going to stop my mama from taking Victoria back to Fresno. Mama talked to me with Fuerza (strong), telling me it was time for me to wake up and stop fantasizing; I was not paying attention to my life and my daughter. Mama was always used to seeing our work and provide for our kids, and she hated to see her children depressed. I had to get up, dust myself off and go back home.

I realized that I was alone with a baby. I got my old job and started back again. I still remember the first time I went out after returning from Mexico. A co-worker and her husband invited me to join them for a night of fun good-all El Torito, downtown Fresno on Tulare St. It was Halloween night everybody was dressed out having fun, I was just observing when suddenly a young man approached me and asked me to dance, I believed he asked me in Spanish, it sounded like, he was wearing a black leather jacket to the waist and black jeans, wearing boots, he had a great smile and seemed nice. His name was John, we danced a few cumbias and soon said goodbye, not before exchanging our home phone numbers, during this time, the cell phone was not so big, like presently. I think the cell phones were selling, but they were terribly expensive.

That same night I met a second guy, he was nice and polite, his name was Martin, he lived in Biola was divorced and live at home with his two daughters. For some reason, he did not call my attention as much as John. I exchanged numbers with him too, I just did not want to say no, but what was worst is that I led him on and went out to dinner one night, and it seemed that he enjoyed my company, that the next day after our dinner outing, he sent me red roses to my work. Well, that same week, I met with John for lunch; we use to see each other for lunch at the Roundtable Pizza near my work over by Ashlan and Fresno Street. John's house was nearby, and he would walk to his house after then. He did not own a car, but he rode a bike and rode the city transportation. To me, that did not seem surprising I owned a car, and I would drive to see him at his house. I did not mind.

Well, I never questioned either why he would drink during our lunch meetings and why when I would go visit him after work, his mom would say he was asleep. Martin, the guy that I met the same night at El Torito, begin to call me more and more, to the point that Mama found out that he the son of a co-worker from the Raisin company she worked. Mama would tell me that according to all the ladies from her work, he was a very nice guy and a great provider. Mama was concerned for me and wanted for me to make a wise choice. Now divorced with a child, she felt it would be hard for me to find a good husband. I was stubborn as always, did not pay any attention to her, and stopped taking a call from Martin.

As time passed, I begin to fit right in with my old employer; his son had come in from the South area and was launching a new business that required my help. My Boss had so much faith in me that he knew I would be a great asset to his son's new business plan idea. And just like he thought I was, I became the office manager of their office, again. I was in charge of hiring and training new personnel in their positions. As well as meeting important people, like attorneys, physicians and marketing coordinator in the media. I was filmed half-hour infomercials to promote the business. When coordinating this infomercial, I met Raul O'Canto he was the marketing representative from Channel 24. Raul was a professional businessman and helped guided my employer with outstanding ideas. Raul and I talked over the phone almost every day and spent time meeting almost one day a week.

I specifically remember one of the lunch meetings with Raul; he invited me to a fine dining restaurant next to his job site. I believe this restaurant is still around; it's now called Steak & Anchor over the Piccadilly Inn across from the International Airport on McKinley and Peach. I do not know if that was the same name for the past nineteen years since the last time I was there. For me, it seemed a bit intimidating; during those times, I was very self-conscious. I felt that this man of so much class wearing a three-piece suit could not be interested in as a woman. As a Mexican woman who really did not know much of table manners and his English was way too educated, he appeared to be a person of great success. I crumbled when he looked at me and said I reminded him of an old girlfriend he once had. He then went on to tell me a little bit about his family and his hobbies. He also shared that he wanted to get to know me, and that is when I closed up. I did not know what to think except to run away from him as fast as possible. I was so nervous and uncomfortable; when our lunch meeting was over, he drove me back to my office, and pretty much after that lunch meeting, I avoided talking to him and he seemed to enjoy my company. I kind of thought our meeting was supposed to be about business, but it was not. So, call it rush or a haze, but I moved in with John. I chose John amongst all the candidates and found out he was an alcoholic with a great big heart. He meant well, but for me, the guy that he was never as good as Joey. After we are living together for about one year, we got married because I was pregnant with what was my fourth pregnancy but my second child. I had one abortion and a miscarriage, both of John's. The abortion happened before John, and I got married; it was one time when he made me so mad after he stayed out the whole night and then came back home still very drunk. Vicky and

I left for Grandma's, and then I went to the clinic to end that pregnancy. Before I could count to 20, I was with John again. I never told him what I did because my intentions were not to return to him. But I guess the sense of me being alone horrified me. Always looking to feel the void space. I now feel bad that I did that because I was so stupid not to do things right. I'm truly against abortions and would never advise my children to do this. I hope God forgave me. It is like I took it out on this defenseless piece of life for making wrong choices. Especially since I returned to the man and later, I became pregnant. But Mother Nature took care of that pregnancy, something happened.

Presently, I think of that when I see my daughters and enjoy them so much that they are alive and can't help thinking, what if I had not gone through the abortion, what if he/she was here, how did he/she would have looked. Even though it has been almost twenty-six years, I can't forgive myself. I suffer as much as my mother since she lost her two grown sons. I can imagine the agony she goes through each day of her life.

When I was with John, I tried to convince myself that he was a great man, that he was what I deserved. However, an inside voice said, "You deserve better." Whether it was my ego or my crazy voice, I do not know. But I had problems accepting this man that he could not put his priorities into perspective. It seemed like he did not even try to stop drinking. If he had stopped, you would say he was a very loving man. He was different than Florencio in many ways because he was not so macho. He was not controlling and loved his daughter from the day she was born. Besides that, he was a very nice man. He was caring and treated

Vicky well. There was one reason why a voice kept me around; God sent us Laura, his family was so happy. God indeed works in mysterious ways. John's dad got to meet his third granddaughter. He died the following year, in February 1995. His dad's death caused John to drink more, I knew that his dad meant the world to him, and he coped with his feelings the only way he knew how. John drank every day after work. By the time 8 pm came about, he was passed out on the couch. He was a great provider; maybe I already said this, but he was. He woke up every morning at 3 am to be at work by 4 am. His job was hard, I did not doubt it; he worked in the freezers at Costco. He did not mess around about his job; he took it seriously. After his dad passed away, our lives together came to an end.

My life with John was still not perfect. Even though this substance abuse disease controlled him, he did his best possible to make us happy. He bought me a house, and we had a dog named White Paws. It was nice, but I could not see myself living with a man who drank from noon till he could no more.

That bad girl attitude at the same time scared came back and broke off the family in the worst possible way. I got involved with a group of friends that were filming some short movies. I was invited to help out with acting some roles, supposedly. Even though I abandoned my dreams a long time ago. I always longed to be involved in these types of things.

All this behavior caused John to get pissed off. John began to question me where I was on the weekends, sometimes gone up too late at night and the girls spending the whole weekend at my mama's house. What was I thinking? Those short stories never got anywhere. All I did, was lost precious time with my daughters. The time that will not come back because they were so young and needed me so much. There are times I wish I can go back and make it right for them.

Before John and I separated, I set up an appointment to get my tubes tied to avoid having more children. Well, I kind of did this behind his back. He accused me of screwing around on him, but I really was not. I just wanted to get as far away from him as possible. I felt like a fish without water. My ego was always telling me that I deserved better than this life. I guess I was just scared of getting pregnant again, knowing that it was going to be a difficult situation.

Our marriage was pretty much over. Once fear was in me, I did not know how to behave. I felt in a way that I was always holding on to my past. I always blamed myself for treating Joey, my ex-boyfriend from Mexico, very badly when I broke up with him the cowardly way I did.

One of the reasons why I opted for having a procedure to not get pregnant, I had my tubes tied. I thought that if this marriage failed, I could take care of two girls but not bring another child.

I was a hard-working person, and I knew that we would be okay. I could provide for them, but no more. I can say it was survival, but now I called it cowardly. I regret what I did. I so wished I would have waited in not making that decision. Well, this marriage ended, and the way it ended was not pretty. I was used to breaking up with guys. Remember, I had experience breaking up with men. Well, it was not that easy; John put up a fight, even though he seemed to not care because that was his way of dealing with things. Well, he showed his true feelings. He did not want to lose his daughter, his princess, his pumpkin. He handled things the way he could, and I handled it the way I could. We had to settle with sharing custody of Laura. It was different than with Florencio; he never even tried to fight for Victoria's custody. Well, thanks to John's sister and mom, Laura stayed close to her dad. Auntie Annie John's sister and their mom, (Sally) Laura's grandmother, have always been there for my Laura. And, I thank them so very much from the bottom of my heart. I apologize for the way I behaved when John and I went through our separation and divorce. I know that they treated me with the utmost respect always. But they knew exactly who the most important persons were, Victoria and Laura. They accepted my daughter, Victoria, as their family, and I will never forget that. They always made her feel comfortable and loved. And even after our separation, Victoria continued to be in their hearts. Thank you, and may God bless you always.

My Awakening

Both my parents are Catholic. I was Baptized and was Confirmed when I was a baby and did my first communion by the time I was eight years old. One thing that I do remember is that when we were growing up, my papa took us to church every Sunday, up until I got married, and then he and Mama were divorced. But, even then, I still kept my faith as a Christian. I raised my daughters to believe in God, and they have been great children to follow a Christian life, as well. I never thought of doing bad things. I avoided having friends when I was older to avoid getting in trouble. I listened to my parents never to use drugs, tattoo, and pierce my body, although, with all the great upbringing, I still managed to mess up my life. I kept dumping one man after the other, trying to fulfill that hole of loneliness. But all I accomplished was a pain to my daughters so much harm. I truly wish I could take it all back, and with a single wish, make everything go away. The best part of all this is that I never lost faith. And, God as my witness, there were times I came close. But He always found ways to put great people in my path. There were many times I considered taking my life but never knew if I could go through with it. I just knew my daughters were the only individuals who could keep me alive.

So, I turned myself over to a psychiatric hospital. It was awful, wakeful, and very scary. Because for a moment, I felt like I would never leave that place. But, after hearing and seeing everything, I can honestly say that I had no problems whatsoever. There were people in there that were, by far, more confused than me. Men who were addicted to medication, young girls who had bulimic disorders, and some people talked of phobias and were afraid of people watching them. What I had was being ungrateful for what I did have, my loving daughters, my terrific mother, and my friends. I thank you, God! But even though I was determined to mess up my life and the lives of my daughters, God did not allow me to do so. He constantly put the right people on my path. Every person that saw the best in me truly did help me. When I was lost, their kind words of encouragement helped me. Maybe not right away, but those words stuck with me like a magic powder, and when it was time, they shaped me into the person I am today.

I pray to God for forgiveness and to grant me the knowledge, opportunity, and time to make things right. I'm grateful to God for all the times He took care of me; he kept me safe in some of the stupid decisions I made and has guided me to take the right steps to correct the harm I have caused to my *familia* (family). Especially to that one individual who, if it were not for her, would never have had the opportunity of all the benefits my children and me both enjoy today. I know I owe my life to both of my parents, but my mama has had so much to do with the woman I am today. All I have to say is that I'm sorry for not responding to her pleadings earlier. When I was young, I was exactly that person she did not want me to be. So, I just have one thing to ask you, Mama, *Perdoname? Si?, Mami por no harber sido obediente, en lo que me decias. Te doy gracias por todo lo que me has dado, por tu gran pacensia y lo que me has ensenado. Te Amo Madrecita.*

Madrecita Mia!

My mama raised me and my brothers and sister pretty much alone. She did the best possible that she knew how. Our Mother saw the vision; she knew exactly what she wanted for us, her children. And luckily, Daniel, my brother, Angela, my sister, their children, me, and my daughters reap the benefits of living in this country. Many people who are in this country illegally suffer because their children cannot go to colleges or universities to continue this theory of "U.S. The land of opportunities." She showed me how to work, how to be strong, and survive in all situations. I admire her way of being; nothing is impossible for her. It was not her fault that I did not study when I was supposed to and turn out as she hoped. But I now have the opportunity to show her that her sacrifices will pay off.

(I wrote this in 2015) Before Graduating from Fresno State. I'm almost forty-nine years of age, and I know that it is too early to celebrate because I still have a ways to go in achieving my lifetime goal of continuing in higher education. But I have to give myself a pat on my back that, for the most part, I'm almost there, and when it's done, I will be so grateful to God as I am right now for allowing me the chance to stick with it and not give up. I think if my mama had been raised in my time or in my daughters, she would have done very well for herself. Mama is very smart.

She's a champion! There is so much that she knows without going to school. She tells me that when she was six years old, she would go to the grocery store in her village and put on credit eggs, flour, beans, and meat. She would then go to the house and cook food for the workers that would pay room and board at Mama Nita's house. Mama only went up to 5th grade; she said that after Mama Nita became a widow, she and her oldest son, Jose, took care of and were in charge of running the farm and land, making sure it ran smoothly. Mama Nita then decided that the daughters did not have to study because they would soon run off and get married, so she would send Mama to stay with one of her brother's houses in a nearby village. Her other sibling's sisters were younger except for the oldest; she was already married and with children. The two brothers also worked the ranch. Mama was not given a chance for education, and when she turned seventeen, she eloped with Papa.

Mama has always been an extraordinary lady. I cannot understand why Papa did not appreciate her and stayed with her for the rest of their lives. However, I do not blame Mama for wanting to divorce Papa. I always did have a good memory, I can remember lots of things except the day I was born, but for the most part, I remember a lot! When I was about seven, my little brother and I slept with Mama, when Papa was working, either in the nightclub or in one of the saloon bars in the Zona Roja, which was the outside of the town, this was where there was prostitution and those types of activities going on. Papa would work there bartending or selling cigarette packs. On that certain day that we slept with Mama, I heard Papa coming in through the front door telling Mama that he was just coming in to take a shower and to get him a clean white shirt; the time must have been like 3 am. I woke up and looked up, looking up. I saw my papa changing and noticed that his neck had some reddish-purple marks. Mama told me to go back to sleep, and when Papa went out the door, I was in the taxi cab waiting for him. I always wondered what had happened to him that night. There were times that Mama seemed very unhappy, but then there were times that everything was okay. Later Mama told me and that Papa used to cheat on her with women from those bars and that she was hoping that after we all came to America, things would have changed, but that was not the case. Papa continued cheating on Mama, and she finally had the courage to divorce him in 1992. Mama had put up with Papa's way of being, I know that he was a very nice-looking man, but Mama was very pretty and smart. Besides being a womanizer, he was a gambler. He played poker at the ranch, and everywhere he would get a chance to gamble, he would be out for up to two to three days, or until the money all went. Mama told me the story when my older brother was about seven months old; her mama had given Papa the opportunity to plant cotton in a small space of her acreage land. Around September, the cotton was picked and sold. Well, Mama put the money away to save, plus she was going to buy some material to make a dress to wear on Mexican Independence Day. Mama was very upset because Papa found the money and disappeared for two days playing (paco) poker. Mama put up with these sorts of behaving for thirty-five years.

I had already filed for divorce from my first husband, my sister Angela had two children, as well. And Daniel had just graduated from Fresno City College. We were her main concerns; she sacrificed herself for us so that we would not go through any mental traumas. I also think she was concerned as to what her mother, sisters, and brothers in Mexico had to say. When she told her mother, Mama Nita, that she was divorcing Papa, she was happy for Mama. She even mentioned to her that it was about time. It is amazing how people change; if Mama had thought of divorcing him at an earlier time, they would have all judged her and said that all she wanted was to be free to fool around with other men. My uncles were pretty close to Papa from the time they worked in the *braceros era.* Maybe, they finally realized that Papa was always a womanizer and the biggest gambler. That's why they did not object to my mama's decision. Plus, Mama had proven to her family that she alone took care of herself; when she decided to cross all of us to America, they did not even bother to ask if she needed help. Instead, they all told her she was crazy, estas loca guera! Mama has always used her hair blonde; that's why she was given the nickname of *Guera; s*he worked hard to raise her children guided us to be good people. My mama has the greatest heart. I thank God because we all have a great heart like hers.

The Past is the Past

Whatever happened in my past is done. I can't erase yesterday, but neither should I ignore it. However, what I can do is not give up on myself. No matter what I have gone through, whether in my native country or in the country I was raised and currently live in, I have the power to accept my flaws and correct them. Yes, moving from one country to another one was not easy. Having to learn a new language and adapting to a new culture was hard also. But the benefits that I have reaped from those things have been tremendously spectacular. I now am the mother of two beautiful daughters who enjoy the same benefits that I have in this country. For example, they speak two languages and enjoy two cultures. I consider myself to be a Mexican American woman; I'm proud that I was born a Mexican and that my mama brought me to this country, the U.S.A., that I refer to like my country. I tell my daughters, always, to embrace their two cultures and heritage because it is one of the greatest inheritances anyone can ever get in life.

Like all people's lives, mine is not perfect, but it has been, by far, most interesting. I have learned through my flaws you will see for yourself that I had many how to make things better for my family and me.

As for my artistic dreams, I had when I was a young girl, I did not reach them, nor did I become a nurse yet. However, I accomplished three years of college and two years in a CSU. This has been, by far, one of my greatest achievements. On my first day in college, I was lost, just like the first day when I attended 4th grade in Sun Empire, the first day I ever came to school in the United States. The only difference was that by then, I spoke and understood English, but it was like if this language was totally different from what I was used to. It was the language from the textbooks that I was not used to. Even though it was somewhat confusing, at the same time, it was fascinating learning. Now that I'm older and wiser, all I'm interested in is finding ways to help my daughters stay interested in school. I always said that I wanted my daughters to look at me as their mentor, model and why not, their hero, too. After all, everything I do is for them. Exactly like my mama, she brought us to the United States to better our lives, and why was I wasting my life busy doing nothing. I now understand my mama's vision. It was not just to teach us to work. It was for us to go further than what she and our father did.

I always admired my female cousins in Mexico, younger and older than me, who went to universities and graduated. I would think that they had more money than us because their parents had the money to send them to school and we had to work and help our parents. And I conformed to that, but always in my mind, I wanted to do better than what I was doing. My parents spoke to us about education and applauded us for going to school and graduating from high school, but it was not required for us to continue our education if we had a job. Which by the time I graduated from high school, I did. My sister Angela had been working and going to school since she was sixteen. She graduated from high school and pretty much stayed working in the same packing-house both our parents worked. At that time, the packing house was called Melikian Packing. It was raisin dehydration and packing. So by the time our youngest brother graduating from high school, he also worked, but was not expected; since he was the youngest, his mother always took care of him. It seemed that after Luis's death, mom became more attached to her only son left. He worked part-time and went to school. There were times that I felt, I don't know if my sister felt this, but I felt that mom protected our little brother more and soon allowed him to do pretty much whatever he wanted, just to please him. But one thing was for sure; Daniel seemed to grow with a different mentality than me.

It was amazing what my younger brother, Daniel did; he went straight into college after graduating high school; even though he did not have a green card, he was a great example of how his mind was not the same as mine and my other siblings, growing up in fear of the culture shock and embarrassed or ashamed of who we were. We were illegally in the country and did not know how to get enrolled in college, and we were afraid of getting rejected.

When Daniel started college, by then, I was two years out of high school and working in a great job. I was always impressed with what our little brother did and always kept that in my subconscious. I tried a few times to return to school, but life always got in my way. The good news is I never gave up. Now I want to lift all younger and older generation's spirits by inspiring that education is essential to learn and better our lives.

There are many opportunities nowadays to continue your education. All a person needs is focus and encouragement from their peers. I want to be part of every person who is willing to make changes like I decided to improve my life for the benefit of my family and me. I asked God to give me the knowledge I needed to accomplish this goal, to be a part of other's lives. If He helps me to succeed, I will have reached another one of my goals.

Getting my Education

Education is a very positive tool in our lives, a proof of our accomplishments; it is definitely one of the strongest and most needed vehicles to achieve our long-term goals. There is so much to learn and to see in this world that God has provided for us to enjoy, which is exactly what I'm doing and will continue to do for the rest of my life. Since 2009, I have been in college. I have traveled across the world with my mind through the books I have read and the research papers I have written. Also, getting to know all the professors, the ones who have shared their life's experiences and accomplishments, alone has been pretty amazing for me. Returning to school twenty-five years later has taught me to appreciate life even more, including when I see all the young students all around me. This has helped me realize that it sure is nice to be young, but it is nicer when you are young, and you know what you want and where do you want to go in life. I find myself amazed by many students because they are so young and smart, and it seems that some of them do not even try hard enough; they give up. I know I always have, even before college, had to try extra hard to get good grades, but one thing I have been persistent. I have to study, read, underline, read again and look up words in the dictionary if I have to comprehend it, but you know what? I do whatever it takes to get there. I'm not ashamed that I'm not smarter than a fifth-grader; as long as I can figure it out, that is what matters to me. Learning has been a challenge for me, and it has great benefits. I say this to myself over and over; if I could go back when I was young and know all that I know now, it would my whole life would have all been different. But you know, the thing that I'm more grateful for is recognizing it. It is never too late; no matter what you have been through, there is always room for improvement. Especially each of you that have the advantage that I did not have when I came into this country, the language, the perfect comprehension of this language. The power of knowledge and believing can take you wherever you want to go; never forget you can have success to your wildest imagination. My daughters and nieces, you have it too because you have the greatest inheritance; you have a great heritage, language, culture, and the will to survive. For most of my life, I let others gear my life. The time came when I just finally got sick and tired.

I remember when I finally liberated myself from the last scum bucket of a boyfriend. I promised myself "no more" there is no one that is going to tell me what to do. I'm the owner of my own life. Today that is what I'm doing. I know what is bad for me and what is good. If I want to take an acting class, karate, aerobics, or golf, I'll do it; if I do not, I won't.

I always wanted to be in love and be loved by someone. But I was not receiving that because I was not prepared for it. I did not even know what I was looking for. I have read more than once that whatever I want, the universe can get it for me. Well, yes, that is true with everything. But there is a thought process that goes along with that. It was up to me to really want it, train my mind to think that I wanted the best for and my daughters. Guess what? The universe did respond. I am with the right person that respects me for who I am. He admires me for who I am and loves me just like the way I am. So that is why I'm ending this book with the story of the man who changed me and my life in the absolute possible way.

Before that, I would like to add that I use to not give myself enough credit for the person who I really was. I did have principles, morals, and good values. But I was confused. Although I lost respect for my body, in a way, I didn't; I have respected myself. I stayed away from drugs; I never stopped caring for myself and my children. I have always been responsible for the wrong decisions I have made. I never blamed anyone other than myself. I can see now how so many young boys and girls get into drugs and in so much trouble by not paying attention to what your mind, heart, and soul really deserve and what one is really capable of being if you just give yourself a chance.

I'm proud that I never marked my body with tattoos that I later would regret. I have nothing against people who do, but I'm just saying that is not the person I am and proud of being conservative in that way. There is nothing wrong with being yourself. I'm not too big on following trends, and who cares if I'm old fashion? Who cares if I'm a square or an edge. I have had my feelings hurt because I talk too much or that I'm awkward and think weird; well, all of that does not matter to me; what does, is that I love who I am. I'm not here to judge anyone or here for anyone to judge me. The day will come when the only one to judge me is God, when I die. Until then, I can choose to listen to the music I want to hear; for example, my favorites are Nicki Minaj, Lady Gaga, Post Malone, and many other famous artists. Does it mean I have to be just like them? The beauty of life is doing what you feel is right for your body, mind, and soul. Yes, one day, my dream is to meet these people, but just because I admire who they are, that does not mean I have to try to look or act like them. These individuals are humans just like me; they have goals, principles, values, and morals like most of us. Being an entertainer is their job, and sometimes they have to go out of the box to make people like them. I applaud them because they each have a wonderful success story, and it was not easy to get where they are now.

Now that I'm near the end of this Memoir, initially, it was for my girls (daughters). To share some of the deep secrets of my childhood and teenage years as a response to their curiosities about my event of losing my virginity. I came to a complete 360-degree circle because just answering their question was not enough. I felt I had to come clean with them and tell them how I felt about it. I share this with one of my friends, and he felt it was a wrong move, but deep down in my heart, I felt it was the right thing to do. I guess it is because I did not want history to repeat itself. So, I wrote a few paragraphs by hand in a notebook. I finally had the courage to let my daughters read it, and I felt awful but relieved at the same time. Now nine years later, I'm writing my autobiography. I started writing it in the middle of 2011; here is the end of 2020, and I have typed over 180 pages. I guess this thought of me doing something has been in me since I was young but didn't know it at the time. Maybe it was this, to write a book, a message to the whole world. My courage to stomp on that pile of fear that was consuming me begins after I returned to school. Every day I sit at the computer and type, I get questioned by daughters and Al, what are you writing? I do not care if they think I'm crazy or do feel I am not going anywhere with this. All I know that nothing and no one is stopping me, "Never again!" I will go to the top from here on out.

All fairy tales end with a happy ending; well, that is what fairy tales are all about, right? And yes, I said at the beginning that this was no Twilight or Harry Potter Story, so I lied. I do feel that everybody's life may be like Twilight or Harry Potter; we can work magic and lots of imagination in our lives. There were times that I felt that I did not belong here; there were many times, actually. Did I use to ask, why me? Why me? But I never could find the answer because I was always thinking the wrong things. I always was asking for more bad things to come to me. I now can compare myself to a drug addict, an alcoholic, and whatever other addictive behavior there is because I was just that, an addict of my own bad feelings. Not until the day came when I was sick and tired of being a failure over and over again. I literally had to kneel down and asked for help. All I ever wanted was to be loved and be treated with respect. I was not a bad person; I took care of my daughters, I worked hard, I was honest, and I felt I deserved a lot better than the scums I had allowed to step all over me. After I divorced John, I became a total "Slut" yes, I admit it because that is what addicts do admit their flaws, and not until they do can they become that person you are destined to be. In my mind, I always wanted to find a man that would love me and respect me, but how could I do that if I was not respecting myself. Before meeting the man of my dreams, I had moved in with two guys. One of them who by far was the worst of all. I was at least ten years younger than him, he did not like to work, I really think he was drug dealing, he was Mexican, he only spoke Spanish, and he was more macho than my first husband; he was calling all the shots with me, he wanted me to be with me where ever I went and would call me at my job every hour. Both of my daughters were younger, and they would adjust to my actions. But my family would see the type of person he was, so they did not trust him, especially Mama; she would not allow my daughter to be around him until I came home from work; she would allow me to pick them up from her house. Now that I look back, I say to myself, "What the heck was I thinking!" I'm just grateful that nothing bad happened to my girls and me.

The other guy that I moved in with was older than me by at least five years; well, this was a real winner, too. That's me being sarcastic. By this, time I was already working as a real estate agent. I met him through a friend. This is the time that I wished I should have been a material girl! I was always a very low-key person, never demanded more than what I had. I always worked and paid for my expenses and never ever expected anyone to take care of me financially, but this time, when I saw what this new guy was doing for me, I said, what the hell, I'll give it a try. I moved into a house in Madera after knowing him for just two months. He paid for the deposit and first month's rent; after that, I was paying for the full rent, and then his brother moved in, too. He and his brother were unemployed, and I was paying all the household expenses. I was cooking three meals a day, cleaning, washing laundry, and working full-time. One day, God sent me a message. I think he said, girlfriend if you do not smell the coffee beans with this, I do not know what will. I went to the casino with my living boyfriend. We decided to leave the casino at about 5 am in the morning. I was driving my 2001 Dodge Stratus. Well, I was sleepy from staying up all night. My daughters had stayed with Mama because my daughters were both older by then, and they hated to live in Madera. So, we are on the Madera Highway 145, traveling Westbound to Madera;

suddenly, I see in my rear-view mirror that a sheriff comes behind me out of nowhere. He pulls me over. I felt confident that I had done nothing wrong; he comes to the passenger's side he asked me for my license and registration. I think he said, "I pulled you over because you were speeding." I did not argue with him because I was falling to sleep. I gave him my driver's license and then went to open the glove compartment, my boyfriend was pressing it to shut with his knee, but I did not know why. So, I pushed so with force, and when it finally opened, a gun suddenly appeared in there. I was in shock. I did not know what to say, and the officer said, "get out of the car," I was standing next to him, and he is asking me questions about the gun. I was not sure how the gun got there, but I had some idea that it belongs to my boyfriend. I said to the officer that I had it for my own protection. I had shot a gun once at a shooting range when I was taking some classes to be a Spanish/English interpreter for law, and our teacher suggested it would be good to learn the sounds of a gunshot to help with our translations. I had borrowed the gun from John's dad, that was like in 1995. But after that, never again had I even thought of owning a gun. You can even imagine how scared I was. It was like my whole blood rushed down to the bottom of my feet. I was pale and sweating at the same time. The officer called in to track the gun; to my luck, it had no history, and I was given a ticket for speeding, for carrying an unlicensed and concealed weapon, plus I was to appear in front of a judge in ten days. When I got in the car, I yelled at my boyfriend. I said, what the hell was he thinking? He got me into so much trouble. I was working on getting my real estate license, it this was something that could affect it.

I know that I was glad I was not taken into custody, but besides that, I had never been involved in any trouble. When this occurred, we had lived together for 8 to 9 months; I had a one-year lease on my name and my brother, so I could not find the property vacant, but he and his brother did. I had no problem kicking them out of the house and my life! Again! I moved back to my mama's house for the fourth time in my life after every time one of my relationships did not work out. I learned harsh lessons like that, thanks to God! I got out of that mess okay; it only cost me $2500 to hire an attorney to defend me and clear my record. I was charged with a misdemeanor, a fine of $300, and one year of probation. On December 5 2003, I was released from the mess I brought on to myself and as well as passing my real estate test. On this day, I was introduced to the man of my dreams. God works in mysterious ways. Because back in May of that same year, finally, I had the opportunity. It just came to me. It was like if I was struck by lightning. I knelt to God and confessed to a priest that I was tired of giving myself to non-sense relationships and one-night stands. I wanted to stop and to meet a man, a nice man, that would love me and appreciate me, not just for once. I told him, "I have always been a good person. My only sins have been sleeping around trying to please man after man to be loved forever and feel good about myself."

He said to me, "Daughter, pray to St. Mary, mother of Jesus and his father and St. Joseph to send you a nice man and before giving yourself to him ask yourself, if God will accept you, with this man in his kingdom." He also said to pray everyday day to receive god's forgiveness. That is how Al came into my life. He is the man that God will accept me in within his kingdom. Well, I should say I'm still working on that. Because in the eyes of God, I'm still married to my first husband, although my heart belongs to Al. But I believe that God will forgive me, and whenever my time comes, he will be there for me.

I used to think that I would never meet a man like Al. I wanted so very much to stop looking. I felt like Juan Gabriel's song, Yo no naci para amar, (I was born not to love). I either did not know how to choose wisely, or I was only attracted to bad boys. I think Alejandra Guzman sings the perfect song about how I felt when I met Al (Mi dia de suerte), my lucky day. I sort of comparing our love story with Bella and Edward from Twilight, except that we have the play roles mixed around because Al is like the good Bella, and I'm thirsty for blood, Vampire. And little by little Al discovered, my flaws. I felt bad because if we did get married, I would not be able to have a child; he would not be able to have a child of his own. But we both needed each other, and we worked through that hurdle. Al accepted me the way I am. He is a great father to my two daughters. Victoria and Laura respect him and see him as a father too. Al was my missing piece to my heart; Al completes me. I needed him, and he needed my love, too.

At first, it was not easy coming to this relationship with so much baggage. But Al made it easy for me because he had a lot to do with my conversion. Yes, he made me human. I actually was the wild beast running around here in there. This part of my life does not make me feel very happy to say about myself. I was pretty bad because, toward the end, I was not even expecting any of them to love me; I just expected them to Smash me, "Like Jersey Shore cast members to refer to having sex." Then I was spitting them out like the beast in Beowulf, but unlike her, I would not put up a fight if they did not want to see me again. I went to the next.

I now think of the damage I was doing to myself; no one was forcing me to do this, and really, I just satisfied the men. As I said, I just satisfied others wildly. I was a wild one, that's for sure. The other occasion was with an old acquaintance's husband; he always had an interest in me, but I never made it obvious to take him seriously, but this one night, he walked me to my car from the club we both happened to be at. We did not see each other it just happened to be that he was there too. I have had some drinks, but I had stopped drinking about one hour before leaving the club, so I was pretty much aware of what was happening. Before leaving the club, we made out, and he offered to take me home. I said no, I glad I had the decency to stop things there.

I have been with my husband for sixteen years; we were boyfriend/girlfriend for almost fourteen years. To this date, we have had a great relationship. I have never ever cheated on him, nor do I intend to ever cheat on him.

I guess you can say that I never really knew what true love was. I always knew that I was not an indecent person, but I became accustomed to the ways of loving them and leave them. Maybe it was my fault that my first marriage failed; maybe it was my fault that my second marriage failed, too. I just felt that with neither of them, I was feeling happy. I was not going to stay around to continue to feel miserable.

I was raised as a Catholic, but there was no religion that I was really following. I was just wildly living.

So, here is Al, A man who is ready to settle down. I was his destiny, and he was mine. "Who knows, he may very well change his mind after he reads this book." Oops! But it will be his decision, and I will respect his decision. Anyhow, we both have so much in common that I felt from day one that he was the one. But he had structure; he believed that only time would tell; he had so much control of his thoughts. Maybe he saw the potential in me because he put in some time to shape me into the woman he always wanted. "I think," he taught me how to laugh, to enjoy life. Never before him would I watch television; not once did I sit down to watch a sitcom. During the time we met, Sex in the City's show was ending. "Sorry, Al," I just ratted out that you watched Sex in the City, so yes, he asked me to come and watch the final episode, but I had no clue who these ladies were? Seinfeld? Who? Never seen one single show, Friends? Whose Friends? "No clue" I'm not trying to be funny; I'm completely honest. I have always been a chatterbox. I would talk away to of how my day went; well, he let me know from the start that he like quiet time. He was pretty set on what he enjoyed. He lived alone for many years, no kids, no one to bother him, so there was the day I would take offense to this, but I would just bite my lip and not say anything. With time I learned to assimilate to him. I now have favorite shows like him. Since we have been together, I became a couch potato, literally, but I can't deny it. It is quite fun. I guessed when I was growing up with my parents; we did not learn to watch television. It was only a few novels a night and off to sleep, work, and school. Then when the time came that I was too busy, raising my daughters and screwing around, literally speaking. I really could not find time to do anything that involved relaxing. Al let time pass just between us; he would invite me over to his apartment because he likes to gather with his friends and barbecue on Sundays while the football games were on. Al is a big-time sports viewer. Yes, I liked sports, but I never watched them, well, except when it was special games like the Super Bowl, World Cup, and the Olympics. The truth is that my daughters and I watch movies, we had all the Disneyland collection movies, and we watch them over, over and over. I was also a soccer, softball, volleyball, and basketball mom. Yes, I took care of my daughters, plus I was always a single mom, so I had to work. I dropped them off at school as early as 7:15 am, and then off to work I went until 5:30 pm, every day that same routine. So, yes, you can say that Al did teach me how to relax. By the time I met him, my oldest was in high school, and my youngest was in 5th grade. Even though I had to look out for my children, it still was not as demanding when they were younger. Also, I was living with Mama, and she helped me look after them, as well that I was no longer working in a stressful job, with an employer that demanded me to be behind a desk for eight hours, with the exception of your thirty-minute lunch breaks and ten minutes intervals. No, I was already working for my own-self, as a real estate agent, I was my own boss, and if I had to see my daughter's volleyball game, I just went without having to fill out a slip to request for time. Overall, Al taught me to believe in myself. I used to feel that I did not deserve good things. I guess that was because I spent all my youth destroying my self-esteem. Still to this day, my family is in shock because they knew my over-turned record with the men in my life. I already told my family that I will not be the only one getting married. In my family, I have been the only party to marry twice. So, now it is somebody else's 'turn' I'm sure my mom and my family are happy as long as I'm happy. And Al has done that and more, for he is the reason I return to school; he heard me mentioned that I had always wished to return to school, and he encourages me to do it. He has helped me to stick to it, and for the first time in my life, I have not given up when being afraid. Al, thank you! So, so much for your support and for helping me find the strength I had lost throughout all those years when I did not know you. God surely did save the best for last. I'm no longer just flying like a leaf with no direction on a windy day. This year, 2020, on February 27, is our 16th anniversary; from then to now, we have lived together in happiness and successfully fulfilling our professional and life goals and dreams. Al and I got married by the Catholic church in the year 2018. My first marriage by the church was annulled by the Catholic Diocese.

I hope you have enjoyed my book. I already apologized beforehand, in case my book in any way offended you. I just feel that there is nothing better than the truth. And with these last words, I would like to end. Always love your body and soul, learn to hear and speak to your heart, keep your feet flat on the ground, and always ask God, or a higher power you believe in, to guide you. Never be afraid of your dreams; go after them; whatever your mind desires can be achieved.

Do not allow anything or anyone to stop you. Remember to recognize your flaws; self-assessment is the hardest but very much needed. Always keep in mind that your mama (Mom) wants the best for you because she loves you no matter what. As a mother, I learned to realize that my actions were out of my mom's control; although she warned me not to get married, not to mix with bad company, I did not listen, and whatever I did, she could not stop it. Just remember, you can fall seven times, but you can dust off and pick yourself self up eight times.

Enjoy life to its fullest; just be kind to your body and soul. Never give up on love. Always ask yourself before giving your whole heart to someone that is promising to love you forever. If this is going to be the right person, ask your heart and listen for its answer. Trust and believe in God. He will guide you to make the right choices, take your time, don't rush your life. You have just read *A Message from a Mother's Heart.*

The End